(1) Do you ever have a struggle with yoursel in the morning?

No
Hardly ever
Yes, but not regularly
Very often   3

(2) If someone offends you, do you complain to them about it?
Yes   0
Probably not, but it depends   1
Probably, but it depends   2 ·
No, never   3

(3) Do you ever say that you will do something, and then somehow find yourself not doing it?
No   0
Hardly ever   1
Sometimes   2
Often   3

(4) 'My head says one thing, but my heart says another.' Is this true for you?
No   0
Not really   1
It does happen   2
Quite often   3

(5) Do you ever have a struggle with yourself as to whether to eat a certain food or not?
No   0
Just occasionally   1
Only when I am on a diet   2
All the time   3

(6) Do people ever get glazed when they talk to you, as if you are boring them, or do they show other signs of boredom?
No   0
Perhaps, sometimes, but not often   1
Yes, from time to time   2
Yes, and I avoid social gatherings for that reason   3

(7) Do you think you have a child of some kind inside you?
No   0
I have thought so once or twice   1
I am pretty sure I have, yes   2
Yes, and it often makes itself felt   3

(8) Do you ever talk to yourself, whether out loud or silently?
No   0
Perhaps occasionally   1
Yes, sometimes, but not regularly   2
All the time   3

(9) 'I want a committed relationship with one person, but I also want my freedom.' Is this true for you?
No   0
Not really   1
Sometimes   2
Often   3

(10) Do you find yourself blaming yourself or criticizing yourself for what you have done?

No	0
I have done so once or twice	1
I have done sometimes, yes	2
Yes, often	3

(11) Do certain words or phrases get you going, wind you up, press your buttons, so that you get really heated?

No	0
Just every now and then, maybe	1
Yes, but not regularly	2
Yes, definitely, often	3

(12) Do you ever find yourself giving the same opinion in the same words as you gave it last time?

No	0
Very occasionally, perhaps	1
Yes, I have noticed that	2
Yes, often, and it bothers me	3

(13) Are you a moody person?

No	0
Not really, not often	1
Sometimes	2
I find moods very hard to shake off	3

(14) Have you ever been aware of one part of yourself taking you over, and acting in such a way as to give you or others hurt or pain?

No, never	0
Maybe once or twice	1
Yes, a number of times	2
Oh yes, all the time	3

(15) Make a list of all the things that you should have done in the past week but did not have time for because you were too busy. Add to this list the other things you would be able to do if you had more time. How many items have you got on your list?

None	0
Between 1 and 5	1
Between 6 and 10	2
Over 10	3

How to score this questionnaire

Write down the figures you got in columns, all the 0s in one column, all the 1s in the next column, all the 2s next to them, and all the 3s in a fourth column.

If your tallest column is 0s, the idea of subpersonalities is not for you, and you are unlikely to get much out of pursuing it.

If your tallest column is 1s, you might possibly be interested, and it would be worth while to persevere in order to see more clearly.

If your tallest column is 2s, you will definitely benefit from pursuing the idea of subpersonalities further.

If your tallest column is 3s, the idea of subpersonalities might overheat your imagination, and that might be dangerous for you. Better not risk it. You might possibly consider going to a therapist instead.

Discover your subpersonalities

Discover your subpersonalities

Our inner world and the people in it

John Rowan

London and New York

First published 1993
by Routledge
11 New Fetter Lane, London EC4P 4EE

Simultaneously published in the USA and Canada
by Routledge
29 West 35th Street, New York, NY 10001

Typeset in Palatino by LaserScript, Mitcham, Surrey
Printed and bound in Great Britain by
Mackays of Chatham PLC, Chatham, Kent

British Library Cataloguing in Publication Data
A catalogue record for this book is available from the British Library

Library of Congress Cataloging in Publication Data
Rowan, John.
    Discovering your subpersonalities: our inner world and the people in it/
John Rowan.
    p. cm.
    Includes bibliographical references and index.
    1. Personality. 2. Multiple personality. 3. Psychosynthesis.
I. Title.
BF698.R88714 1993
155.2–dc20   93-14812
                                                       CIP
ISBN 0–415–07366–9

Contents

Introduction
Let us call them subpersonalities

Are we just one person, just one self? Or do we have several little people inside us, all wanting different things? Why should we take it for granted that we have just one personality? Would it not make more sense to say that we are many? Maybe we have more than one centre within ourselves.

Maybe our minds are naturally divided into portions and phases. Maybe they have earlier and later historical levels. Perhaps there are various zones and developmental strata. And maybe this leads to many internal figures.

Can we not find within ourselves an impish child? Is there somewhere a hero or heroine? Sometimes a supervising authority? Sometimes a nurturing parent? Perhaps even sometimes a psychopath who cares nothing about others? The list could go on.

If we can come to realize that each of us is normally a group, maybe that would be quite a relief? I may get visual impressions of the people inside me, and that wouldn't worry me any more. I may sense that I am hearing their voices, and that wouldn't panic me, either. I may talk with them and they with each other without any of this being abnormal in any way.

And in terms of everyday life, this is a reassuring thought for many of us. How often have people said, 'Talking to yourself – first sign of insanity', and put someone into a panic? It is true that at certain stages of senile dementia, talking to oneself may be the first sign of insanity, but for most of us it is a normal daily occurrence. Our experience contains the unity of the one without losing the possibilities of the many.

If we recognize the people within us we can give them some space. And if we give them the right to be there, we can get to know them better. And if we can get to know them better, we can get in more control of our own lives. We can call them subpersonalities, and learn more about them. Our everyday experience is very much concerned with subpersonalities already; it is just a matter of recognizing and allowing this fact.

Psychologists have investigated the maturing of the ego. They have found that at the lower levels of maturity, everything is black or white. We are either all good or all bad. Other people are either all good or all bad. But at the higher levels of development we can begin to recognize and face our own internal conflicts. We can accept the idea that we may have both good and bad within us. To deny any internal conflicts bespeaks a lower level of personal growth.

The man who always has to know the answer to everything is a bore, and a bully, because he is avoiding his weaknesses. The woman who never knows the answer to anything is avoiding her strengths. They are neither of them doing justice to the whole person who is really there.

The person who says 'I am all good' is just as immature and inaccurate as the person who says 'I am all bad'. We are all mixtures, and one way of looking at this which can be very revealing is to give each part of the mixture a voice and let it talk to us. In this way we can find out more about ourselves and explore our inner world.

SOME EXAMPLES

Little Sally is an angel at home and a devil at school; Johnnie is a devil at home and an angel at school. Many parents have found this kind of thing to be true.

It is a common experience to hear someone talking over the telephone in a certain voice, and when coming off the phone to talk to someone in the room in a quite different voice. Some people actually have a 'telephone voice' which they cultivate; others do it without thinking, quite without any intention of changing their voice at all.

It is well known that people often become much more aggressive when they are behind the wheel of a car. The role, very masculine as it normally is, brings out the inner aggression. This aggression might normally be hidden or suppressed or diverted.

Someone who repeats the same phrase, the same sentence, the same story over and over again may become a bore. It is easy to see that when someone else is doing it, much harder when it is ourselves; yet most people are guilty of it at one time or another. It is as if we are taken over for a time by the person who always says these things.

In the same way, we may find ourselves doing things or saying things we did not mean to do – 'I don't know what came over me!' These are the times when we may be aware of one of our subpersonalities taking over.

One very common form of this is when we say 'Yes' when we really mean 'No', or when we do not complain when our toes are trodden on. Our inner desire to please takes over and makes us weak.

TAKING OVER

So in everyday life we have many examples of another personality taking over at times, or having some influence on our lives. This is the basic idea we shall be playing with in this book: that we have more than one personality inside us. Once we can understand this and accept it, it will give us much more control over our own lives and our own destiny.

In novels, we are given many examples of all this, as for example in *Les liaisons dangereuses* by Choderlos de Laclos, published as long ago as in 1782:

After supper, by turns childish and sensible, crazy and serious, sometimes as sexy as I pleased, I enjoyed thinking of him as a sultan in the middle of his harem, where I was by turns each of his different favourites. In fact, his repeated overtures, although always sent to the same woman, seemed each time to be received by a new mistress.

This playful sense of being able to move from one personality to another is not uncommon in our experience. But of course it can be much more serious than that.

HOW MANY?

People have wondered how many people we may have inside us. My answer is that there are usually between four and nine such

The
Telephone
Voice

people. More than nine and I begin to suspect that some of them are simply aspects of others, and should be grouped with them; less than four and I begin to wonder whether there has been sufficient attention paid to the less visible ones. We shall return to this in Chapter 18.

In each one of us we can find some of these semi-autonomous subpersonalities striving to express themselves. By saying that they are semi-autonomous, what we mean is that they have a life of their own, but they are not completely separate.

So one of the easiest and most basic ways of gaining more access to our inner resources is to get to know our subpersonalities. Some of the names which have come up in people's self-examination include the Hag, the Mystic, the Materialist, the Idealist, the Pillar of Strength, the Sneak, the Religious Fanatic, the Sensitive Listener, the Crusader, the Doubter, the Grabbie, the Frightened Child, the Poisoner, the Struggler, the Tester, the Shining Light, the Bitch Goddess, the Great High Gluck and the Dummy. Many others are possible.

PUTTING THEM IN ORDER

Some people, of course, have not been able to resist the temptation to give some order to these subpersonalities. If we put some of these orderings together, we get a list of common subpersonalities. Not everyone has all of them, but they are very commonly found.

The Protector/Controller

This arises early in development, and consists of that part of us which tries to fit into the parents and what they want. It notices what works and what does not work, what pleases and what does not please. It erects a rigid set of answers to these questions. It learns how to protect our vulnerability. This is the one which keeps the subpersonalities hidden most of the time. Can combine with the Critic.

The Critic

This is the one which tells us we have got it wrong. It is extremely acute, and notices everything which could make us feel rotten

about ourselves. It delights in using its power. It can combine and co-operate with other subpersonalities very well. It can be masculine or feminine, and may be given names such as the Prosecuting Attorney, the Slavedriver or the Big Shot.

The Pusher

This is the one which tells us that we have not done the chores, written the letter, done our exercises. It appears to be on our side, reminding us of our duties when we might forget. But in reality it is not helpful in its present form. We have never done enough. As soon as we cross an item off the top of the list, the Pusher will add one on to the bottom. Can combine with the Critic.

The Perfectionist

Insists on the highest standards. Cannot stand the second-rate, the shoddy, the messy, the incomplete, the shapeless. No mistakes should be made. Again claims to be on our side, but it does not work positively. It always puts us down. Can combine with the Critic.

Central Organizing Subpersonality

Examples are the Executive Self, Big Eggo, Chairman Self, or Co-ordinating Self. In some personalities, the Chairman may be weak, and the power of leadership may be in the hands of the Critic or some other subpersonality. In other personalities, the Executive can be too strong, and dominate everything else. This may also be called the Audience subpersonality, or the Other People subpersonality, or the Ego. Kept in the right proportion, this can be a very valuable subpersonality.

The Inner Child

This can take various forms – the vulnerable child (often extremely sensitive), the playful child, the magical child. It may be too young or hurt to use words. We shall look in more detail at the inner child towards the end of Chapter 4.

Good, Socialized, Adapted Child

This is the obedient, conforming Child Self who tries to please authorities. Some of this is necessary for socialization and in co-operative working with others. Too much of this subpersonality inclines the person towards over-conformity, rote obedience, and lack of creativity. Has also been called the Performer or the Pleaser. It is the one who says 'Yes' to everyone's demands, and tries to make them happy. Very often covers up for anger. Very nice, but compulsive about it, and unable to be anything other than nice.

The Little Professor

This is the child who must have an answer to everything, but who jumps to conclusions without having enough evidence to make a proper decision.

Natural Child

This inner child is usually creative, may be nonconforming and rebellious. It carries much of the spontaneity and playfulness of the original child you once were. Can also offer a kind of creativity, based on not knowing what is possible and what is impossible. A sense of humour often comes with this sub-personality. Again, unfortunately, this one sometimes gets lost, but it can be found again and restored to life.

Nurturing Parent

This is in charge of supporting, giving love, care, attention, praise and positive reinforcement. Other names for this character include Protecting Parent and Guardian Angel. It is a sad fact that this useful subpersonality has sometimes got lost somewhere in the life of a particular individual, and time and trouble has to be taken to get it back again.

The Power Brokers

Have to do with Power, Ambition, Domination, Money, Selfish-ness, all seen as subpersonalities. Very often these characters may cover up for more vulnerable subpersonalities.

The Shadow

What we would least like to be like. Our own negative self-image. This may take various forms, the most common of which are the Nasty (the Nazi, the Punisher, the Hater, the Bully, etc.), the Weak (the Wimp, the Yielder, the Nothing, the Ineffectual, etc.) and the Vampire (leading on and then destroying, seducing and then killing, attracting and then dumping, etc.).

MEN AND WOMEN

What we can notice about these is that they all assume that all subpersonalities apply to men and to women equally, or just the same. But this is not true.

The Power Brokers are heavyweights, and are much more likely to be found in men. The Pleaser is more likely to be found in women. But women these days want power too, not just a dependent relationship with people who do have social power. The kind of power they are seeking is also somewhat different; not so much the old parental kinds of power, but more power plus vulnerability – what is nowadays often called empowerment. We shall have more to say about this in Chapter 19.

Bill is a bully at work and meek at home; Tony is meek at work and a bully at home. This also is pretty frequent.

CAN BE USEFUL

This sort of thing can be used in counselling or psychotherapy, and we shall be coming to that in later chapters. But in everyday terms we know very well that it is not only battles between two aspects of ourselves which happen inside us. We often seem to incorporate three, four or any other number of selves. Some will be isolates and others will work in teams. Some will appear in many circumstances and others only on a few special kinds of occasions. Some will be more powerful and others will give way to them. Sometimes, people can offer and use quite elaborated accounts of their 'community of selves'. This immediately gives us a common-sense perspective for looking at these matters.

Few of us are the same when talking to our bank manager and when talking to our children.

SPECIAL NOTE ON THE EXERCISES

These are all contained within boxes, so that it is quite clear what is an exercise and what is not.

Exercises like those in this book are regarded as common property, and are not protected by copyright. They are the equivalent of the methodology of a scientific experiment: any scientist can repeat the experiment and it is considered a virtue in science to replicate other people's experiments. Each exercise is different each time it is done, and you can also feel free to alter anything that seems to you not well stated or worked out, or that has to be adapted to a particular situation.

It is a good idea to have a notebook by you when carrying out any of these exercises, so that you can write down any insights you get, and remember them better.

Some of them can take you into deep psychological water, and if you find yourself getting upset, you may decide to give up that exercise for the moment. However, if you are in a counselling relationship, or in psychotherapy, or in a growth group, etc., it is better to go ahead with the exercise, and feel as upset as necessary, and take your feelings forward for fuller understanding. These upset feelings are the gateway to your soul, and if you treat them in this way they can be very useful to you in your development.

A BASIC LIST

Write a list of all your subpersonalities, those you are aware of at a conscious level right now. Give each a name, and write about five lines describing that one. It is all right to write more if you feel like it. Keep your first list and look at it once every three months or so, and add to it or modify it in any way that seems right.

Chapter 1

Where do they come from?
Roles that we play

Where do subpersonalities come from? One of the six main
sources of subpersonalities is to be found in the roles that we
play. We are all familiar with roles such as father, housewife,
stockbroker, actress, butcher, solicitor or unemployed person.
Such examples have been studied in role theory, and is has been
found that we can get so much into a role that it becomes hard to
get out of again. Some roles are notorious for this.

TEACHER

The role of teacher is hard to switch off, and many teachers go
home and hear the words, 'I'm not one of your pupils, you know,
don't talk to me like that.'

There is a real temptation to carry on with the same actions at
home as worked well at school.

SOCIAL WORKER

Similarly with social workers; there seems to be something about
being a social worker which is very seductive and enticing. Many
social workers go home and hear the words, 'Don't you casework
me.'

A certain way of talking to people and being with people
becomes a sort of second nature.

MOTHER

The role of mother is notorious for its trapping qualities. After
having been 'Mum' for twenty years or so, the children leave

social worker

at Home

at Work

home, and, if no other role can be found, the woman is left with an emptiness which is hard to fill. She may compulsively go on being 'Mum' in all sorts of situations where it is not the best thing for her to do.

EXAMPLE

A classic in the study of roles was the investigation by S. Lieberman some years back, where attitudes towards union and management were obtained from 2,354 rank-and-file workers in a factory.

During the year, many workers changed roles, some becoming foremen and some becoming shop stewards for the union. Now basically foremen look up to management and down on the union members; while in contrast shop stewards look up to the union members and down on the management.

The new foremen changed their attitudes so as to become more favourable towards management and more critical of the union; the new shop stewards changed their attitudes also, so as to become more favourable towards the union and more critical of management. These attitude changes occurred soon after the role changes, and within three years the two groups of men had developed almost diametrically opposite attitudes.

It happened, two years later, that fewer foremen were needed in the plant, so that eight of them were demoted to their former positions. These eight were therefore compared with twelve other foremen who continued in that role, and it was found that their attitudes had changed back to what they were originally. It is quite clear that their attitudes followed the roles they played, as role theory would predict.

What we are saying here is that if you play a role in society, you develop a subpersonality corresponding to that role.

HAVING MANY FACES

Suppose we take a student at university named Anne. We might say that there are many facets and sides of Anne. In fact, there are many Annes that different people encounter. She is a Madonna fan, a conscientious student, a snotty spoiled brat, an insecure little girl, and so on.

She might say something like this: 'There are so many different

FOREMAN

SHOP STEWARD

mes that I am confused about who I really am. It seems that I change according to who I'm with: My parents think I'm really hard-working and dedicated to getting good marks and doing well. My friends think I'm a real party girl. And I don't know who I think I am.'

This again is a common enough experience. We can put it down to adolescent identity problems. Of course, adolescence is a vague period of time – it is hard to know when it has finally ended; maybe it doesn't end at all for some people.

EXPERIMENTS

What we are saying, then, is that we are all very familiar with the idea that people can behave very differently in different circumstances. Psychological studies have shown this very clearly. We do modify our self-presentation in different situations. But we are often quite unaware of what we are doing, and it feels to us as though we are being sincere and retaining our integrity all the way through. Really the individual has many potential selves. We carry within us the capacity to define ourselves as warm or cold, dominant or submissive, sexy or plain, with many or few resources. The social conditions around us help determine which of these options are evoked.

For example, in an experiment carried out by Kenneth Gergen, eighteen women college students were interviewed by another woman. Every time the student gave a self-evaluation that was more positive than the average, the interviewer showed signs of approval: nodding, smiling, murmuring agreement. But for every answer which was answered more negatively than the average, the interviewer frowned, shook her head or murmured disagreement. It became clear to the student that the interviewer took a very positive view of her. And as a result of this, the self-evaluative statements of the student became gradually more and more positive.

To check up on this, the student later filled in a series of self-ratings which were not seen by the original interviewer. And there were significant increases in self-esteem as measured in this way.

The people we are with affect us, making us feel more like our best self or our worst self.

Barbara Wishnow did an experiment where young women

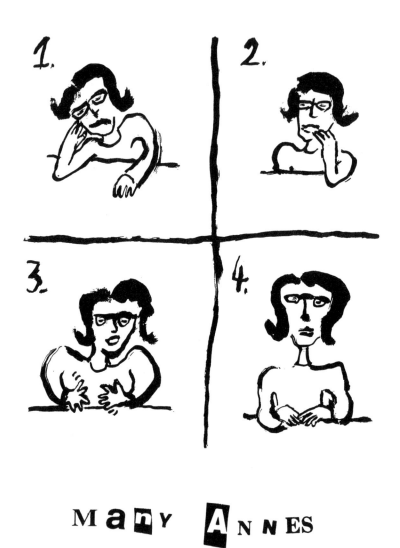

MANY ANNES

college students were asked to write self-descriptions to be shown to a fellow-participant in the role of a partner. Half the students were given a negative description of their partner-to-be. It showed this partner to be a whiner, unhappy, ugly and intellectually dull. Her childhood had been miserable, she hated school and was intensely fearful about the future. The other half of the students in the experiment were given a positive description of their partner-to-be. This showed the partner to be cheerful, intelligent and beautiful. She loved school, had had a marvellous childhood and was optimistic about the future.

What were the results of this experiment? The students who read the first description wrote their own self-descriptions in a self-deprecatory way, admitting to many shortcomings they had not previously mentioned; it was as if they were saying, 'I know what you mean, I have problems too.' But the students who read the second description wrote about themselves that they had many good qualities they had not mentioned before, and they mentioned very few negative qualities; it was as if they were saying, 'You think you're so great, but I am pretty terrific too.'

Yet when asked later whether they had modified their self-presentation at all under the influence of the partner's description, 60 per cent of the students said that they had been completely consistent, and had not changed in any way. In reality, of course, they had taken up a role in relation to their partner.

Another study asked male applicants for an interesting and well-paid summer job to fill in many tests, including a self-evaluation questionnaire. It was explained that their responses to this questionnaire would have nothing to do with their chances of being hired, but that honest answers were needed in order to construct a good test. As each applicant sat there working, the experimenters sent in another young man, supposedly another applicant for the job.

In half the cases this man was Mr Clean: he wore a well-tailored business suit, gleaming shoes and carried a smart attaché case, from which he took out a dozen sharpened pencils and a book of Plato. In the other half, this man was Mr Dirty: he wore a torn sweat shirt, trousers torn off at the knees, and a day's growth of beard. He had no pencils, only a battered copy of a popular novel. Neither of these men spoke to the original applicant.

What effect did these visitors have on the self-evaluations being filled in? Mr Clean brought about a sharp drop in

self-esteem – the applicants felt sloppy, stupid
intimidating character. Mr Dirty brought abo
self-esteem – the applicants felt more handsom
optimistic. In another similar experiment, 75 p
applicants felt they had been completely accurate
their self-evaluations, and had not been influenced ii

THE FACES WE PUT ON

This has also been brought out in the work of sociologists who have
studied impression management. We all create impressions of
ourselves, and also try to create different impressions on different
people. In one study of the Shetland Islands, for example, when a
neighbour dropped in to have a cup of tea, he would ordinarily
smile as he came into the cottage. There were no hiding places
outside the cottage, so the people inside could see the visitors clearly
as they approached. They could see the visitors drop whatever
expression they normally had, and replace it with a sociable one just
before reaching the door. However, some visitors, in appreciating
that this was going on, would blindly adopt a social face a long
distance from the house, thus making sure that their image was
constant.

These social faces are of course very common and may be quite
transient. What we are more interested in, in this book, is the
more long-lasting face which we may take into numerous
situations. Such faces can sometimes be extraordinarily powerful.

TEN LEADING CHARACTERS

Make a list of about ten (can be more, can be less) well-
known people who stand out for you from the past or
present, fact or fiction, some good and some bad. When you
have come to the end of the list of people who are significant
for you in this way, write an adjective against each one – a
word which describes their character or what they stand for
in your estimation. Now imagine that each of these is one of
your subpersonalities. Does this make sense? Stay with each
one for a while, and muse on how this one may be playing
a part in your life somehow – maybe too much, maybe too
little, maybe just right.

(1) Do you like answering questionnaires?
    Yes, if they make sense   0
    Not very much   1
    I think questionnaires are boring   2
    I hate questionnaires   3

(2) What do you think of being grown up?
    It's all right, quite normal   0
    I sometimes resent the demands   1
    I don't know if I really want to be grown up   2
    I don't like being grown up   3

(3) Do you feel as if you are creative?
    Not particularly, no more than anyone else   0
    Occasionally I do   1
    I can be creative when I want to be   2
    Yes   3

(4) How much of the time are you bored?
    Not often at all   0
    Some of the time   1
    Quite often   2
    Very often   3

(5) How important to you is it to have fun?
    Just occasionally, as a contrast to real life   0
    I like to have a fair amount   1
    It is important   2
    It is very important   3

How to score

This is to discover whether you have a Free Child sub-personality.

0–5   You do not have much in the way of a Free Child at all, and this may make you rather staid and boring. Why not try to cultivate your Free Child a bit more? Everyone around you would benefit from this, and you too.

6–10 You do have a Free Child, and it is in a modest position, not too suppressed and not too wild. Cultivate it wisely.

11–15 You do have a Free Child subpersonality, and it is very well developed. Just watch out that it does not take over too much.

Chapter 2

How we do battle with ourselves
Internal conflicts

We have seen, then, that roles can be a source of subpersonalities.
What other sources are there?

One of the most important sources of subpersonalities is the
way in which we can have inner conflicts – that is, conflicts
between two or more of our subpersonalities.

To see how complex this can become, consider for example this
quotation from Barry Stevens in *Person to Person*:

> In the beginning, I was one person, knowing nothing but my
> own experience.
> Then I was told things, and I became two people: the little
> girl who said how terrible it was that the boys had a fire going
> in the lot next door where they were roasting apples (which
> was what the women said) – and the little girl who, when the
> boys were called by their mothers to go to the store, ran out
> and tended the fire and the apples and loved doing it.
> So then there were two of I.
> One I always doing something that the other I disapproved
> of. Or other I said what I disapproved of. All this argument in
> me so much. ...
> The most important thing is to have a career. The most im-
> portant thing is to get married. The hell with everyone. Be nice
> to everyone. The most important thing is sex. The most important
> thing is to have money in the bank. The most important thing
> is to have everyone like you. The most important thing is to
> dress well. The most important thing is to be sophisticated and
> say what you don't mean and don't let anyone know what you
> feel. The most important thing is to be ahead of everyone else.
> The most important thing is a black seal coat and china and

silver. The most important thing is to be clean. The most important thing is to pay your debts. The most important thing is not to be taken in by anyone else. The most important thing is to love your parents. ...

Suddenly: 'What am I doing?' 'Am I to go through life playing the clown?' 'What am I doing, going to parties that I don't enjoy?' 'What am I doing, being with people who bore me?' 'Why am I so hollow and the hollowness filled with emptiness?' A shell. How has this shell grown around me? . . . I refuses to play the clown any more. Which I is that? 'She used to be fun, but now she thinks too much about herself.' I lets friends drop away. Which I is that? 'She's being too much by herself. That's bad. She's losing her mind.' Which mind?

Is this still the voice of the adolescent? Or is it not rather the voice of all of us? When we are seriously and touchingly concerned by the manyness of the I, and by the falseness of the I, in a much more adult and existential way?

SPLIT IN TWO

Most of us have probably, at some time, found ourselves talking or acting as if we were two people rather than one. We talk sometimes of being in 'two minds' about something, one part of us wanting to do one thing and another part wanting to do something else. Quite often we hear people talk of having to 'do battle' with themselves, as if one aspect of themselves was in conflict with another.

One of the commonest of these splits is between the topdog and the underdog. The topdog says things like, 'Why haven't you done it yet?' The underdog says things like, 'I will do it, just give me a chance.' This argument goes on and on, and has been called 'the famous self-torture game'. We shall see later how this can be changed.

MANY VOICES

It was during a time of painful conflict that I first began to experience myself as more than one. It was as though I sat in the middle, surrounded by many selves. Some tried to push me one way and some another. Each presented a different good argument and none of them would give the others an opportunity to be fully heard. While I listened to one and then the other, the conversation outside me went on to other things, and none of my selves were able to speak up because of the competition inside me. To others I seemed sometimes far removed, and it was true. I had been called away to attend to an inner meeting – the voices of my own many selves.

So we are not speaking here merely of different roles which we may take up; we are also talking of internal conflicts which are giving us trouble in one way or another. One woman in a research group I led found that she had two subpersonalities: one was called Can't Cope, and the other was Bill the Jailer. Can't Cope wouldn't let her wash up the dishes, and Bill the Jailer wouldn't let her go out of the house without washing up the dishes. So she wandered around the house, not being able to wash up the dishes and not being able to go out either.

THE INNER CRITIC

Think of a time when you put yourself down, or criticized yourself, or beat yourself over the head for something you did or failed to do. Write a dialogue between the one who criticizes and the one who is criticized. (You might spend about 15 minutes on this.) Does this look familiar? Does it go somewhere and get resolved, or is it an eternal game that just goes on and on? If the latter, ask the critic: 'Where do you come from? When did you arrive? What do you want? What do you need?' And write down the answers. Then ask the same questions of the one who was criticized. (You might spend 15 minutes on this as well.) Then go back to the original dialogue, and see if you can now give it a better ending.

PARTS OF THE BODY

Also under this heading come those times when our bodies, or parts of our bodies, seem to act as if they were our antagonists. They, too, can be regarded as subpersonalities with motives of their own. Supposing I have a pain in my shoulders. I can, if I wish, talk to my shoulders and ask them what they are trying to

express through this pain. If I let them reply – and we shall see later exactly how this is done – then they may say that I am taking on too many burdens, more than they can carry. I can then learn from this, and perhaps give some of my tasks to others, or refuse to take them on in future.

TALKING TO THE PAIN

Take a physical pain which you have in your body – it may be a headache, or a pain in the shoulders, or in the stomach – it does not matter. Get closely in touch with this pain. Now talk to it, saying whatever needs to be said – statements, questions, demands, anything at all.

And now be the pain. Just take a moment or two to get into the feeling of being that, instead of being you. You are the pain, talking back to the questioner. As you talk back, just answer with whatever comes from that position.

When that seems to come to an end, go back to being yourself, and see if there is anything further to say – any further questions or demands or whatever it may be. Keep on with this dialogue, negotiating if necessary, until some resolution appears. Don't be afraid to talk to yourself in this way – it is quite all right.

We shall come back to this in Chapter 15, where we go into the whole question of how this kind of dialogue is carried on fruitfully.

Bill the Jailer

ANNA

Can't Cope

(1) Do you think that you are basically an impostor, and that if people really knew you, they would not be taken in by your apparent successes?

No	0
Only occasionally	1
Sometimes	2
Most of the time	3

(2) Do you think it is better to discount your own abilities, because then pride does not lead to a fall?

No	0
Occasionally I feel like this	1
Yes, modesty is a good thing	2
Sometimes I think I do it too much	3

(3) 'If things are going too well, I worry about what is going to happen next to spoil it all.' Do you agree?

No	0
Only rarely	1
Sometimes	2
Usually	3

(4) 'I feel I can't do anything right at all.' How often do you feel like this?

Never	0
Occasionally	1
Sometimes	2
Often	3

(5) 'Life is hard and always will be hard. Basically you can't win.' Do you agree?

No	0
Occasionally	1
Sometimes	2
Yes	3

(6) Do you find yourself blaming yourself or criticizing yourself for what you have done?

No	0
I have done so once or twice	1
I have done sometimes, yes	2
Yes, often	3

How to score

This is to discover whether you have an Inner Critic sub-personality.

0–6   You do not have an Inner Critic, or if you do it is well hidden or under control.

7–12   You do have an Inner Critic, but it does not cause too much trouble, and you can probably live with it all right.

13–18 You have a problem with your Inner Critic, and need to do some work to correct this, otherwise your life will be a misery.

Chapter 3

Creating them to order
Possible selves

If roles and internal conflicts are important sources of sub-personalities within us, what other sources may there be? One important source is our own ideas about how we wish or want to be.

HEROES AND HEROINES

We may identify with a hero or heroine, or with an admired group, and take on their characteristics. For example, in the 1970s I frequently came across hippie and revolutionary subpersonalities in the people I was working with. People identified with these characters, and knew how they dressed, how they behaved and how they talked. Even if they only did it at weekends or on demonstrations, they knew how to be this type of person.

Some sociologists have suggested that heroes and celebrities are used in a search for identity. These fantasy images may come from the past, as well as from the present. We have all seen the 'wannabe' who wants to be like the latest pop star, and dresses just like they do.

POSSIBLE SELVES

Some researchers in psychology have shown that the idea of 'possible selves' can help us. If we want to understand people's commitments, this can help us. If we want to understand how people are going to shape up in the future it can help us. These researchers found that students who had a definite idea of the person they would be like at the end of their course at college did better. They came out higher in their examinations than those

who did not. They were also more likely to complete the course and not drop out before the end. This is very interesting stuff.

CREATING SUBPERSONALITIES

Some psychotherapists can deliberately set up within themselves a fantasy image of the client, so as to be able to tune in to the client better; this is the deliberate setting up of a subpersonality for the purpose of developing resonance with the client.

Actors of the 'method' school work by setting up within themselves a subpersonality corresponding to the character they are playing. This is sometimes so successful that they find they cannot switch off when they get home, and they carry on acting like the character instead of like themselves.

I once saw an artist trying to create certain movements in a cartoon character. He put himself into the same position as the character, and used his own movements in that fantasy situation to learn how to draw the character.

Most of the time, of course, it is not done in this deliberate way, but rather as an attempt to live up to some ideal, which in this case takes the form of an individual.

USING MODELS

In recent years there has been a good deal of interest in deliberately tuning in to imaginary helpers of one kind or another.

Robert Bly has written about the Wildman, the fierce character covered in hair who lives inside every man, and whose strength can be drawn on in a positive way. Many men have found great benefit from going to workshops where this character is honoured. I myself have written about the Horned God as an image helpful to men.

In the case of women, the Warrior has been a character who has been found to be of value. This kind of energy has been unavailable to women until recently. It was considered unfeminine or even castrating. One can see clearly, however, how necessary it is for self-protection and how powerless a woman can be if this energy is disowned.

Warrior energy is needed by all humans, both men and women, for self-protection. Needless to say, women are seen as life-givers and healers, and the thought that they might have any

destructive energies spreads panic among the population. To be denied access to the destructiveness in oneself is to be denied another major power source.

POWER ANIMALS

Nowadays there is a great deal of interest in shamanism, and shamanic workshops are offered all over the place. One of the things that happens at such workshops is that you are invited to get in touch with your power animal. This is the animal which is meaningful to you as a symbol to learn from. By getting really in touch with this animal, you can turn it into a subpersonality, talk to it and take instruction from it. This is well worth while, and a fascinating thing to do.

TWO-PERSON DIALOGUE: TEN QUESTIONS

Write a dialogue between any two of your subpersonalities. Make sure to include anything that they like or dislike about each other. If they turn out to be opponents, try taking each one separately after a while, and talking to it individually, perhaps asking it the questions mentioned in the previous chapter. Other questions which it may be good to ask individually include the following:

What do you look like?
How old are you?
What kind of situations bring you out?
What is your general approach to the world?
What is your basic motive for being there?
What have you got to offer?
What are your blocks to full functioning?
What would happen if you took over completely?
What helps you to grow?
How do you relate to women/children/men?

After asking such questions of each one separately, it often makes sense to go back to the original dialogue and complete it – it may be much easier to work with now.

Chapter 4

Delving deeper
Our personal history

The fourth way we can set up subpersonalities within us is through our personal history, starting with our earliest experiences. In order to understand how this can happen, we have to realize that we have as it were two minds. There is a conscious mind, which uses language, makes rules, understands figures, and so on. There is also an unconscious mind, which works rather differently and quite out of our awareness.

We are now going to be talking about some of the most difficult subpersonalities. But it is crucially important to understand how they are formed. Otherwise we can never change them, and they often do badly need to be changed.

THE PERSONAL UNCONSCIOUS

As we shall see in more detail in a later chapter, there is a long history of ideas about the unconscious mind, starting from the ideas of Mesmer and the hypnotic tradition in the eighteenth century.

But in this century the great thinkers about the unconscious have been Freud and Jung. And it was Freud who suggested most clearly one process by which a subpersonality can get set up.

It is interesting to see exactly what Freud says about the super-ego, which answers very precisely to our description of a subpersonality. Freud says that in the first instance our mothers are very powerful figures in our world. They have the power to give and the power to take away. They can reward by their very presence, and punish by their simple absence. This absence can be very painful, and it is in order to avoid this pain that our unconscious mind may resort to the defence of introjection.

What introjection means is that we take the external object and the feelings and images associated with it (in this case the mother) inside us, so that we will never be without it. In fantasy we incorporate the mother into ourselves. Then when we want to know what to do, or how to feel, or what to think, we can consult as it were the inner mother instead of waiting to hear what the real mother will say or do.

So at first it is as if we have swallowed whole the mother, and now we have an internal mother who can be consulted or responded to. As time goes on, the boundary between us and this internalized mother gets thinner and thinner until it disappears altogether. At that point we do not have an introjected mother any more: we have a superego, a conscience.

The conscience now carries on the work which the mother used to do. We have internalized her view of the world and it has become our view of the world. And what may happen is that we then split the world into two – the good and the bad. The conscience then becomes the automatically good, and we erect an opposite, the tempter. We now have a new kind of self-torture game consisting of the struggles between the conscience and the tempter.

Now in later life we may question this automatic conscience derived from the mother, but that is a conscious questioning done at the level of language and everyday understanding. It does not affect the unconscious processes which were set in motion so early in our lives. The conscious mind, so to speak, inhabits one world, but the unconscious mind inhabits a different world. There is no necessary alignment between the one and the other. The decisions we make at a conscious level do not necessarily get through at all to the decisions made at an unconscious level.

So the internalized mother, which Jung calls the mother complex, still keeps on telling us what to do and what not to do, and how to feel, and what images to have, as if nothing had happened. The struggle between the conscience and the tempter may then go on as before.

In other words, we have taken inside us a voice from our external world, and internalized it. An important point, however, is that the term 'introjection' is often regarded in rather too simple a way. It assumes that one is incorporating into the personality something that is outside the personality. But in reality, of course, we can only take in what we understand, as we understand it. So

tempter

conscience

what is introjected to form a subpersonality is not the mother as she is to herself, or as she is to other people, but the mother as she is for the infant. It is certainly not the mother as she is today, in the everyday world.

But this means that the infant can only incorporate the mother's attitudes in so far as it is capable of having these attitudes. It will incorporate its own version or experience of these attitudes. So what is incorporated will be essentially what the infant is and what is being projected on to the mother. This is a complicated idea to grasp, but what it is saying is that the mother we incorporate is very much our own version of the mother. It is a version of the mother which we have helped to create by our own perception. It is the way we see the mother, through our own private spectacles.

We have already seen (in Chapter 3) how important this is, because other projections from our own fantasy life can also give rise to subpersonalities. And this explains why our brothers and sisters may have very different ideas of what our mother was like. Our mother is our mother; their mother is their mother.

Eric Berne caught the mood of this whole idea very well when he talked about everyone having within them internalized parent, adult and child ego states. It was he who first stated very clearly that the Critical Parent and the Nurturing Parent may get quite separated until they seem like two separate subpersonalities. Classically, the mother is more likely to the model for the Nurturing Parent, and the father the model for the Critical Parent, but it does not have to be like that, and there can be many exceptions and variations.

PARENT DIALOGUE

If there is something you want to deal with in relation to your parents, here is one exercise to help with that. Sit quietly, relax and take a few deep breaths. Imagine one of your parents sitting facing you. Notice how they are sitting, what they are wearing, what expression they have on their face. The image you get may be of them in recent times, or may be of some years back. Just go with whatever comes, and if this makes you some other age, be that other age.

Start talking to them. Don't censor it, just let whatever wants to come out come out. Express yourself with feeling, don't hold back on the emotions. Be completely honest and say all the things you wanted to say but never could, positive and negative. (If very powerful feelings come up, you can choose to come back into the here and now, and return to the exercise another day; or you can choose to stay with your feelings.)

Now be your parent. Respond to what you have just said. Tell your child how you feel about it, and how it was for you.

Change over again: what do you want to say now? How do you respond to what your parent told you? How do you feel towards them now?

Now tell your parent what you need from the relationship. Make a demand, as directly and specifically as you can.

Become the parent again. How do you respond? What do you want from the child?

Change over again and respond as yourself. Carry on with the dialogue as long as it takes to arrive at some better understanding and an agreement as to how things will be from now on.

SPLITTING AND INTROJECTION

Now when a subpersonality is set up in the way we have discussed, it is very often as a response to a situation of panic. In our original example, it may have been panic that the mother was never coming back, or it may have been some other panic.

Protector/Controller

Introjection, or some other unconscious defence mechanism, is then used to deal with the situation. If this is successful, then this defence is then used in other, similar situations.

The subpersonality we call the Protector/Controller may arise at this point.

The Protector/Controller says that the person (the infant) is basically inept, weak, powerless, and so forth, and so it would be better if the Protector/Controller were given complete charge of everything. The Protector/Controller in reality, of course, is no more able to cope than the supposedly inept one. But it knows how to throw up defences against panic, which may be successful in the short term and potentially crippling in the long run. So here is another division within the person which can be very important in later life.

It is important to recognize that the events we are talking about here may be very unimportant to the adults, and very important to the infant.

Let us suppose that the feeling of the mother's existence lasts a few minutes. If the mother is away more than that few minutes, then the image of the mother in the mind of the baby fades. The baby is distressed, but this distress is soon mended, because the mother returns in a few more minutes, and the image is restored. In this few more minutes the baby has not become altered. But suppose that the mother's absence goes on for longer than the baby can stand, and the image of the mother goes missing altogether. The baby now feels completely lost. At that moment the distress turns into panic. The unconscious slips into gear, so to speak, and starts to defend against this trauma. After those extra minutes, after that panic, after a trauma, the mother's return does not mend the baby's altered state.

Trauma implies that the baby has experienced a break in life's continuity. The defences of the unconscious mind now become organized to protect against this. There may be a terrible fear. Or there may be an acute confusional state. A panicky confusion can feel to the baby like complete disintegration because of a very young and still forming ego structure. A subpersonality may come in to provide the answer. This is called splitting, because the original person (baby, infant) is now split off from the subpersonality.

So if we are right, we can see how not only in the very first experience of trauma, but also in the later experiences of trauma, this defence can result in the setting up of more and more subpersonalities within the person.

This is how the internal objects mentioned by the object relations school get set up. The introjected figures are called internal objects because we relate to them, emotionally and impulsively, in the same ways as we do towards externally real persons. The only difference is that, just because they are internal, we relate to them in higher degrees of intensity. The formation of this inner world of internal objects and situations proceeds from the very beginnings of life.

Each subpersonality that is set up represents a decision – 'this is the way to lead my life' – often made in a hurry and on inadequate evidence. Some of them are complete introjects – someone else's way of being is swallowed whole.

THE INNER CHILD

Choose a particularly traumatic period of your childhood. This may be a time when something happened which anyone would think was severe, or if you didn't have anything like this, so far as you know, it may be just some occasion when you were not appreciated, not treated properly, in some quite mild way.

Sit quietly, relax and take a few deep breaths. Imagine yourself as you were then, in as much detail as you can manage, as if that child was in front of you now. Then, talk to the child that you were. Say any words that come to you. Offer any advice. Be the good adult that you wish you had had. If it feels right, take a cushion or pillow to represent the child that you were and hold it, stroke it or rock it. Say and do whatever feels right to you, for as long as it feels right, and then say goodbye.

THE COEX SYSTEM

Stanislav Grof casts a flood of light on this whole area by his notion of the COEX system (system of condensed experience). He shows how the trauma can be represented again and again in the life of the person. Later experiences may bring back the original feelings.

A COEX system can be defined as a specific constellation of memories consisting of condensed experiences (and related feelings and fantasies) from different life periods of the individual. The memories belonging to a particular COEX system have a similar basic theme or contain similar elements. This means that they are going to be associated with a strong emotional charge of the same quality.

For example, suppose that I have a painful experience – my partner leaves me, let us say. If that represents a COEX for me, then I am not only going to have the pain of the moment. I am going to add to that all the pain of the previous experiences like that. The earliest ones may be to do with my mother, and be quite traumatic. So now all these old tapes are playing, so to speak, and adding to my present pain. This intensified pain may be quite unbearable. So now I do not just have a painful experience, I have an experience of Primal Pain. That is how it works.

I once worked with a woman named Carmen, who was very afraid of her father in real life. She did not see him very often, but when she went to see him, he could make her feel completely powerless and unhappy. This looked like a COEX system to me, so I encouraged her to go back and explore it.

It turned out that behind her father was the priest. In her childhood the priest had been a powerful figure, who had seemed to her the very essence of power and authority. So the power of the priest reinforced the power of the father, and made him many times more powerful.

But it then turned out that behind the priest was the church. This, in her mind, was an immensely powerful worldwide and all-wise, all-knowing organization, and again the power of her father was reinforced. And behind that again was the Pope. To her the pope was infallible, all-powerful and generally unbeatable. So her father's power was strengthened once again. And behind this, deepest of all and highest of all, was God. She saw God as an omnipotent, omniscient Father-figure, quite unquestionable and unsurpassable.

It was not surprising, therefore, that she had such strong feelings about her father. As we started to unravel the strands of this COEX system, it turned out that many of the beliefs which constituted it were highly questionable, and that she had in fact questioned them over the years, but it was necessary to go back and re-examine them *as a child, as they felt at the time, when these feelings were strongest*. She was then able to let go of those of them

GOD

The Pope

Church

Priest

Father

Carmen

that were merely oppressive and indefensible, and this led to her being able to face and deal with her father.

The deepest layers of this system are represented by vivid and colourful memories of experiences derived from the panics of infancy and early childhood. More superficial layers of such a system involve memories of similar experiences from later periods, up to the present life situation. So there is a kind of ladder of COEX experiences stretching back down into the past. Each COEX system has a basic theme that permeates all the rungs of this ladder and reveals what they have in common.

If we personify a COEX system, it comes to life as a subpersonality. As we saw earlier, the introjects start off by 'riding herd' on one of the subregions, telling it what to and what not to do. Then they move inside the subregion and become a part of it. This can then lead to a topdog/underdog split inside the subregion affected.

THE INNER CHILD

The personal history of each person starts far back. Childhood is an impressionable time. This means that much of what goes on in us under the surface has to do with the inner child. This is the child who was suppressed as we grew up. In adolescence we say to ourselves: 'When I was a child, I spoke as a child, I understood as a child, I thought as a child: but when I grew up, I put away childish things.' But again this is done at a conscious level, and at an unconscious level something quite different is going on. These things which are put away are only put away in a drawer, so to speak; and they are still there, still there in the drawer.

So in our unconscious minds there they are – the children we disowned and did not want to know about. The child decisions, the child feelings, the child panics. But they can still affect us, because they still need to be heard. If we do not listen to them and pay proper attention to them, they can sabotage us or punish us or give us pain in various ways.

They can take many forms. We looked at some of these in the Introduction, but here is the fullest list which has been put together as far as I know:

The Adapted Child (Compliant Child), who always wants to be liked, and will do anything to get approval from almost anyone. As we saw, this can develop into a full-blown Pleaser subpersonality, who is quite compulsive about being nice to everyone and never upsetting anyone by saying 'No'.

The Natural Child (Free Child), who is quite spontaneous, and knows how to have a good time and enjoy life. This can be a great source of joy and liveliness if not disowned as too dangerous.

The Little Professor, who has to have answers to everything, and jumps to conclusions in the absence of evidence on which to base an answer. There can be more than one form of this, and some people have talked about the Mischievous Gamey Little Professor and the Creative Inventive Little Professor, who is a bit different. Again this is only dangerous when compulsive.

Sleepy (a primitive, highly dependent part of the inner child), who just wants to latch on to someone and go to sleep in their lap. Again this is perfectly legitimate and proper at times, and trouble only comes when it is disowned and fights back.

Spooky (that part of the inner child concerned with symbolizing), who often feels very scared because of seeing hidden meanings in everything. Can also be very valuable as a source of intuitive sensing, because of this capacity for seeing images and sensing meanings.

The Adapted Critical Child, who criticizes everything, but without the knowledge to do so well, so always gets into trouble. Really just needs to grow up, but panic prevents this.

The Disturbed Natural Child, who has a strong desire to be spontaneous and fun-loving, but who somehow always gets it wrong. Again just needs to grow up in a safe environment, which is what it never had. The early trauma may have been something quite bad and harmful, such as sexual abuse, which could be hard to get at.

The Vengeful Child, whose main motive is revenge, but who does not have much idea of how to go about it, and may not be able to admit that revenge is what it is about. So it can lash out in sometimes quite subtle ways – little teasings, little putdowns.

The Self-Protective Child, who is always looking for safety, even at great cost. May use quite drastic and unsuitable measures to get its own way. High level of panic means that some very early trauma may be involved.

There is a lot of talk these days about the child within, and many books and workshops deal with such issues. But some of them seem quite oversimplified, as if there were just one inner child

THE SELF - PROTECTIVE CHILD

and just one way of dealing with it. There may be more than one, and this must be kept in mind.

AN EXAMPLE

One thing which needs to be said positively about these inner children is that they know how to 'be'. Most of the rest of our personality knows how to 'do' and how to 'have'. If we want to understand how to work in any way with these inner children we must learn how to 'be' with them; otherwise they cannot emerge. When dealing with the inner child, the dictum is: 'There's nowhere to go and there's nothing to do.'

For example, let us look at a case where a woman had been sexually abused as a child by her father. She went to a humanistic psychotherapist. After quite a bit of other work had been done, in which the woman had learned how to 'be' with the therapist, she was asked to return to the time her father had molested her sexually, and simultaneously to observe the scene as her adult self. The scene was played out without the therapist intervening, up to the moment at which the child was ordered to her room after the abuse was over. At this moment, the therapist asked the patient to enter the scene in her adult self, meet her child self on the stairs, pick her up, comfort and reassure her, and generally to act as she would to any child in such a situation. She was asked to continue this until the child was reassured and at peace, and then to return to present time. The patient reported that she had done this, and that she felt that the child had heard her, and had responded to her, and had begun to feel much better. Perhaps more important was the feeling that she could recognize in her adult self that her child self was in fact innocent.

This example shows just one way of working with the inner child, and there are many others, as we shall see later.

ANOTHER EXAMPLE

But many other things can come from our personal history besides our inner child. For example, one person discovered inside himself a very nasty subpersonality, like an animal living underground and very reluctant to expose itself. This man was encouraged to have a good look at this character, and when he did so, he found what seemed to him a monster. His whole image

of himself as a decent, good person collapsed. It was a filthy creature, with green eyes and a mean disposition. It was only because this man had a sense of personal centredness, which he had derived from earlier work on himself, that he was able to confront it. Without this, he felt he would have been afraid that it was all he was, that it would overpower him, and so on. But with a therapist's encouragement, this man went on to bring this character out into the open and have a dialogue with it. As time went on, he began to see it in quite a different light.

He began to see that if he had not possessed that subpersonality, derived from his early fantasies, he would have dropped into all kinds of trouble. Though the creature first emerged as nasty and sneaky, at bottom it was only trying to say 'No' when the man was always and automatically inclined to say 'Yes' to everyone and everything.

This underlines an important point: there are no good or bad subpersonalities, though they very often appear to us in the first place as good and bad pairs. All subpersonalities are expressions of vital elements of our being, however negative they may seem to us at first. This is a most important truth. Subpersonalities become harmful only when they control us, and this usually happens when we are unaware of them.

REWRITING THE STORY

If there is some particular incident from your childhood which seems to stand out, and you want to deal with it, here is an exercise which can help. Write the event down like a short story in the present tense, told from your point of view. Try to remember what happened as accurately as you can. Reconstruct the dialogue. Record your feelings.

Then rewrite the story the way you would like it to have happened. Bring in other characters if necessary, or change the existing characters. Give yourself added boldness or ingenuity if necessary.

Or love the person whom you neglected. Whatever you wish. Create new dialogue. Record your new and changed feelings. Invent your ending and resolution. Don't stop until it is as you want it.

(1) Do you like answering questionnaires?

I hate questionnaires	0
Not very much. Sometimes I do.	1
I think questionnaires are interesting	2
I love questionnaires	3

(2) If someone asks you for directions will you tell them the way, even if you don't know for sure?

No	0
Very rarely, I might	1
Quite often, yes	2
Every time	3

(3) Somebody you value asks you the answer to a question. You know you have the answer somewhere at home. How long would you go on looking for it if you couldn't find it at first?

Half an hour or less	0
More than half an hour but less than one hour	1
More than one hour but less than two hours	2
More than two hours	3

(4) Someone asks you the time. What do you say?

It's about a quarter to four	0
It's three forty-six	1
It's fifteen forty-six	2
It's fifteen forty-six and thirty seconds	3

(5) 'Every problem has an answer.' Do you agree?

No	0
I hope it's true, but I'm not sure	1
Probably	2
Definitely	3

How to score

This is to discover if you have a Little Professor subpersonality.

0–5   You do not have a Little Professor, and there is no particular reason why you should.

6–10 You do have a Little Professor, but this part of you is quite well under control. Watch out for it taking over any more.

11–15 Your Little Professor is a little bit too well developed, and could cause you trouble. See if there is some action you can take to reduce it.

Chapter 5

How society tells us we are no good
The patripsych

Let us now look at the fifth origin of subpersonalities. Here we leave the personal unconscious and come on to the cultural unconscious. This is something shared by all those who share in a common culture. The common culture we all share today, in every developed country in the world (in virtually all the less developed countries too) has been named as patriarchy – that is, a hierarchical arrangement dominated by men. This is an oppressive system based upon domination of the weaker by the stronger. The basic outline of this arrangement has been clearly set out in the diagram from Elizabeth Dodson Gray.

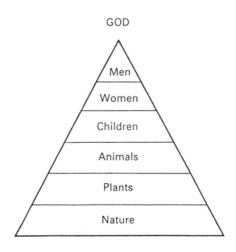

The world map of patriarchy (After Elizabeth Dodson Gray, *Patriarchy as a Conceptual Trap*, Wellesley, MA: Roundtable Press, 1982)

As can be seen from this diagram, there are a number of layers in the hierarchy, and the rule is that each layer can exploit and use everything on any layer which is lower down. So the plants can exploit inanimate nature (rivers, mountains, soil, etc.), the animals can exploit the plants and nature, the children can exploit the animals, the plants and nature, and so on up the scale. And if we want to know what God thinks about all this, we have to ask the men, because they are the closest to God, and they know.

If we want to know what to expect and what is basically allowed in our society, we can consult this diagram. But we are now going one step further, and saying that because we are brought up in such a society from our very earliest times, and it is impressed upon us by so many of our personal experiences, this structure becomes internalized. It becomes, inside us, the cultural unconscious.

THE CULTURAL UNCONSCIOUS

This is what has been called the Patripsych – the internal hierarchy which matches the external hierarchy. It has been called a constellation of patriarchal patterns. By this we mean all the attitudes, ideas and feelings, usually compulsive and unconscious, that develop in relation to authority and control in a society like ours.

Now because boys and girls are brought up differently, and with different expectations and life chances, men tend to internalize mastery and control. They assume that they will be at the top of the pyramid. If this position is threatened, they will automatically act in order to restore the hierarchical order.

Women, on the other hand, tend to internalize self-effacement and dependency. Deep down, it is impressed upon them that theirs is not the top position, and that they will do better to establish a good relationship with someone who is at the top. Even when they reject this at a conscious level, the cultural unconscious will often catch up with them. So women not only have many practical obstacles to reaching positions of real social power in our society; they also have an internal saboteur helping to stop them.

THE PIG PARENT

In the 1970s, this was being studied by a group connected with Claude Steiner in San Francisco. At the time they called it the Pig Parent. This is not a particularly good title now, because it was based on the slang term for an oppressive type of policeman, and we have moved on since then. But this title does make it clear that what we are dealing with here is an internalized form of cultural oppression. It is the voice within us which says that hierarchy is the only right way of organizing, and patriarchy the truest form of hierarchy. And it is a parental voice, in the sense of a voice which has authority and which thinks it is right.

It has been found that in women's groups, women can become familiar with what insidiously keeps them down. First of all, there is the obvious, overt, male supremacy which many people are already aware of and may be struggling against. But secondly, and perhaps more importantly, there is the oppression which has been internalized. It is this internalized oppression which turns women against themselves. It causes them to be their own worst enemies rather than their own loving best friends. It is the expression of all the values which keep women subordinate.

The idea of the Pig Parent is again an internal pattern of responses – the voice within us which tells us that we are no good, that we need good, pure, strong figures to lean on and depend on and admire, that we can never make it on our own, that it is wrong to aim at equality.

THE PATRIPSYCH

The patripsych (pronounced pay-tri-syke) is another and perhaps more defensible term for what we have called the internal constellation of patriarchal patterns. This development is closely related to learning about sex roles – learning about whether you are a little boy or a little girl. The patripsych says:

> I am your superior. I am right, and you are wrong. I know what you should be like, you do not. I am dominant, you are submissive. I talk, you listen. I am adult-like, you are child-like. I am good, you are bad. I lay down the image, you must live up to it. I know what's best for you, you do not. I can deal with life, you cannot. I am masterful and competent, you are not. I am substantial, you are empty. I exist, you do not.

This is really a crippling voice, and it runs right through our society, affecting us all in one way or another.

- It is the patripsych I have to contend with when I experience compulsive feelings of dependency on authority figures, so that I assume they know best. I want to get near them. I want to be like them, and so forth. The only safe place is under their shadow.
- It is also the patripsych I have to contend with when I have a compulsive need to fight authority figures, opposing them regardless of what they do, dedicating my life to their destruction and seeing them as symbols of evil. The only safe place is total opposition.
- And it is the patripsych I have to contend with when I am withdrawing into myself, refusing to compete, being uncommunicative, not engaging in any way and in this way avoiding all the issues of control. The only safe place is a position of powerlessness.

These three patterns are ways of relating to the patripsych, and defending against the emotions which it arouses in us.

INNER COMPULSIONS

It is important to remember that we not only develop compulsive ways of relating to people who are in authority over us but also develop compulsive ways of relating when we are in positions of authority ourselves. The general point about this is that it is very difficult for anyone to relate to authority, whether it be our own authority or the authority of others, in a healthy and non-compulsive way. We are more compulsive than we think, and power relations can then get mystified and confused.

The patriarchal family continues to exist, even though the outward appearance of many families may be relaxed and equal. This usually becomes more apparent when children are born, and the crisis of parenthood pushes men and women into more one-sided roles. People who thought they could be equal when they were just part of a couple find themselves lapsing into unequal roles once children come along.

This kind of insight may remind us of the extraordinary way in which patriarchy has entered into our language and our thinking at deep unconscious levels.

THE SELF-HATER

Another version of this has been described as the self-hater. The self-hater is the inner representation of oppressive power – the kind of power which dominates, and which goes with the pattern of hierarchy which we have been identifying. We have internalized it, not just from our parents, but from every institution in society with which we have contact. It is the structure in the psyche that perpetuates domination. It reminds us of our helplessness, our powerlessness. It blames the victim; it tells us we are bad when bad things happen to us.

And this applies to men just as much as to women. Both men and women have internalized the oppression of a patriarchal society, and both have this internal voice. It is just that society tells men that they have to be leaders, and so they lead, but still with the voice telling them that they are no good, that they are unworthy, that they have no right to be equal or to be loved for themselves. And so they perpetuate the structures which will make it all seem impersonal and objective, and nothing to do with them personally.

A DREAM

This example will illustrate the way in which we can recognize the patripsych when it comes up in our dreams. An older man dreamed that he was in his old school – an ancient school, with wood panelling and big separate desks with heavy hinged lids, and a raised dais for the master. Somehow he found himself being the walls of the room, and saying to the boys in the class:

> I am here to make you feel small. I am here to put you down. I am here to make you feel so weak and inadequate that you will latch on the words of the master as being your only hope. I am here to reduce you to obedience to the master. I am here to make sure that you understand the conditions under which you can progress – my conditions. And if you rebel, I am here to make sure that your rebellion is futile and pointless.

MASCULINE BIAS

There is a mocking, masculine tone to this speech which often does appear in the words of the patripsych. This is the authentic

voice of oppression, which in our time means patriarchy. It is patriarchy which produces all the typical forms of oppression which we meet with today – racism, classism, adultism, sexism and all the rest. And it produces a certain way of thinking, which has been called masculine bias.

Masculine bias appears in our behaviour whenever we act out the following categories, regardless of which element in each pair we are most drawn to at any given moment: superior/inferior; dominant/submissive; master/slave; butch/femme. All of these false dichotomies are inherently sexist, since they express the desire to be masculine or to possess the masculine in someone else.

Under patriarchy, it is the stereotyped masculine qualities which get all the acclaim and all the interest, and this is true both for men and for women.

It may be remembered that Freud said that women suffer from penis envy, and these ideas about masculine bias begin to sound rather similar, except that we should talk rather about power envy. And except that we now see it as applying to men as well as women, and as being much more complex: we may want to be close to male authority; we may want to oppose it; we may want to withdraw from it. But each time this is not a real choice – we do it in a compulsive way, driven by unconscious demands.

THE PATRIPSYCH IN THERAPY

It is extraordinarily difficult to deal with the patripsych in therapy. All the most successful attempts seem to have been in groups, rather than in one-to-one work. This is simply because as fast as we break down the patterns in our therapy sessions, society tries very hard to put them back again. If we really want to deal with the patripsych, it seems that we have to set up some kind of living community which will have different values; but then it seems that we lose all power to change the broader society. At least we have to learn to talk to one another about these things, and to realize that we are not alone with them.

Ultimately, then, we are faced with the answer that in order to deal with this aspect of therapy thoroughly, we have to change the whole society. If this is true, this is a very important area of study, and one where it is well worth while to sort out one's own attitudes. In Chapter 9, we shall be looking at this question in a more practical way.

A DREAM CHARACTER

Pick out a striking character from one of your dreams, and write a dialogue with this character. (It is a good idea to keep a dream book if you can.) There is no fixed length for this – let it go on as long as it needs to, and if at the end it seems unfinished, feel free to come back to it later and write some more. Is this character one of your subpersonalities? Is it related to the patripsych in any way?

QUESTIONS FOR WOMEN

(1) In a large organization, the man at the top is replaced by a woman. As a worker in that organization, how does this make you feel?

Just the same, or pleased	0
A few questions might go through my mind	1
I would feel a little bit uneasy	2
I would feel quite uneasy about it	3

(2) 'Women can do far more behind the scenes than by competing with men.' Do you agree?

No	0
It does seem to be true, sometimes	1
That is my experience for the most part	2
Yes, and I wish this were recognized more widely	3

(3) If there is a larger and a smaller portion of some delicious and nourishing food, and you are sharing the meal with a man, who would you serve with the larger portion?

It would depend	0
I would be inclined to let the man have the larger one	1
I would give the larger one to the man	2
The man should obviously have the larger portion	3

(4) You go in for an examination, and come out top. You have achieved a remarkable score which is quite unusual. The news spreads far and wide. How do you feel?

Marvellous	0
Good, but a little bit nervous	1
Quite nervous and unsure as to what it means	2
Definitely worried and uneasy	3

(5) People often say that you are beautiful, but you know you have one physical feature that is not as it should be. How do you feel when people compliment you?

Good	0
I just hope they are not being patronizing	1
I wonder what they really think	2
They are obviously lying, so I don't respect them	3

How to score

This is to discover whether you have a Patripsych.

0–5   You have become aware of the Patripsych, and it is not causing you any problems at the moment. But watch out, it is subtle and pervasive, and could return in some other form.

6–10   You do have a Patripsych, and it needs to be watched, because it can cause problems.

11–15 You are strongly under the influence of the Patripsych, and it may make you very unhappy if you do not do something about it.

QUESTIONS FOR MEN

(1) In a large organization, the man at the top is replaced by a woman. As a worker in that organization, how does this make you feel?

Just the same, or pleased	0
A few questions might go through my mind	1
I would feel a little bit uneasy	2
I would feel quite uneasy about it	3

(2) If someone asks you for directions will you tell them the way, even if you don't know for sure?

No	0
Very rarely, I might	1
Quite often, yes	2
Every time	3

(3) 'The main job of a man is to be a breadwinner. Anything else on top of that is a luxury.' Do you agree?

No	0
I think there is something in it	1
Basically, I suppose, yes	2
Yes, and I wish more people realized that	3

(4) Do you think a man should be able to keep his head and know what to do in an emergency?

Not necessarily	0
It would be nice to think so	1
I suppose so, yes	2
Definitely	3

(5) Do you think a man should really take responsibility and not shirk getting into positions of power?

Not necessarily	0
Ideally, yes	1
Yes, I think so	2
Yes, and I do this myself	3

How to score

This is to discover whether you have a Patripsych.

0–5   You have become aware of the Patripsych, and it is not causing you any problems at the moment. But watch out, it is subtle and pervasive, and could return in some other form.

6–10   You do have a Patripsych, and it needs to be watched, because it can cause problems.

11–15 You are strongly under the influence of the Patripsych, and it may make you and others very unhappy if you do not do something about it.

Chapter 6

The deepest level of all
The collective unconscious and archetypes

There is one more source of subpersonalities we have to consider. This is what Jung called the collective unconscious. Many people have added to the idea since his time. The collective unconscious is the source of very powerful images which are common to many societies, many times and many places.

We have already noticed one of these images – that of the Shadow, who we met in the Introduction. Another important image is that of the Anima, the woman who lives inside every man, and the Animus, the man who lives inside every woman.

ARCHETYPES

Jung called these images archetypes, and suggested that they came from inside us, rather than from outside us. This does not mean, however, that they are inherited in the genes. It would make more sense today to think in terms of Rupert Sheldrake's idea of morphic resonance. This is a wide-ranging theory which shows how such images might be handed down to us. This theory says that once a pattern of human action has been set up, it becomes easier to repeat that same pattern. Somehow the shape of the pattern becomes easier to pick up, as if it were now in stock, so to speak.

These images can be personalized, sometimes as subpersonalities, sometimes as gods and goddesses; their myths are archetypal stories. They evoke feelings and images, and touch on themes that are universal and part of our human inheritance. They ring true to our shared human experience; so they seem vaguely familiar even when heard for the first time.

The word archetype is well chosen, for *typos* means something that makes an imprint or pattern. And so arche-types mean the ancient, primordial patterns that are impressed on the psyche. They come as a result of the age-long experience of life that people have passed through. The collective unconscious is composed of, or contains, these archetypes. They are patterns of psychic energy. Jung has compared them to the axis systems of crystals, which determine the form and structure of the crystal even while the salt is in solution.

For example, one of the most common archetypes which comes up in psychotherapy is the Shadow. The Shadow is that part of ourselves which we like least. In other terms, it is the negative self-image. It is what we are afraid we are like, underneath the covers and the pretences. As we saw briefly in the Introduction, for some people it is nasty – 'If they knew how full of hate I was, how evil are my wishes, how vicious I really am, they would all reject me.' For some people it is weak – 'If they knew how inept I am, how incapable, how lacking in all positive qualities, they would all reject me.' For others again it is more complex – 'If they knew how I put on a friendly face to allure people, and then when they are hooked I turn on them and destroy them, they would all reject me.' So the Shadow is that part of us we would least like to meet. We shall see later that the Shadow is not in fact all bad, but has something to offer us that is positive.

Another archetype is the Persona. The Persona is that part of us we would most like other people to meet. It is the public-relations self, the mask we put on to greet the world. It has been said that in Jungian therapy there is often a movement from dealing with the Persona at the start of the therapy, to the Ego as the second stage, to the Shadow as the third stage, then to the Anima or Animus, and to the Self as the final stage. Some would interpose the Wise Old Man and the Wise Old Woman as spiritual archetypes coming before the final step of the Self.

But here we are not trying to be pure Jungians, but to see how the archetype can be a separate and distinct origin of sub-personalities. It seems to make sense to me that some of the things we come up with in working with people seem to be very generally applicable. In other words, they are common to more than one person. Some of these, in turn, seem to be common to more than one culture. And it is these universal subpersonalities which I think it makes sense to think of as archetypes.

In this sense the parent, adult and child ego states which we have met before can be perfectly well understood as archetypes. Even in cultures where fatherhood was denied or not understood, a child would still have parents. Similarly, it would make sense to say that the Protector/Controller was an archetype, since all cultures have some such notion. This makes it obvious that archetypes are in fact very common; but as Jung says, when they come up, they come up with power and fascination.

THE SOUL

It is important to remember that archetypes tend to be metaphors rather than things. We find ourselves less able to say what an archetype is literally and more inclined to describe them in images. We can't seem to touch one or point to one, and rather speak of what they are like. Archetypes throw us into an imaginative style of discourse. In fact, it is precisely as metaphors that Jung – who reintroduced the ancient idea of archetype into modern psychology – writes of them, insisting upon their indefinability.

Let us then imagine archetypes as the deepest patterns of psychic functioning, the roots of the soul. As such we are often struck by their emotional possessive effect, the way in which they take us over. Some say that an archetype can best be compared to a god or goddess. It is less accessible to the senses and to the intellect than it is to the imaginative vision and emotion of the soul.

So we do not look for biological explanations, which perhaps could be seen as a reductionist way of going on, but rather trust to the mythopoetic mind itself as its own explanation. We may prefer to speak of the archetypal matrix in which we are all embedded – archetypes are not things which we have, but more like a sort of home in which we partake.

EXAMPLES

But it is not only gods and goddesses who can be perceived and treated in this way: there are many archetypes, and today there are a number of writers who are treating them as important. For example, several people have written at length about the importance of the four archetypes King, Warrior, Magician and Lover for understanding men, and the maturity in men.

A God & A Goddess

Some have written about goddesses and the ways in which they enter into the lives of modern women. The love goddess Aphrodite, the virgin goddess Artemis, the wifely goddess Hera, the homely goddess Hestia, the dark goddess Hecate, the warrior goddess Athena – these can all be inspiring for women at different times in their lives.

Carol Pearson has given us a great deal of information and help in tackling twelve archetypes: the Innocent, the Orphan, the Seeker, the Lover, the Warrior, the Caregiver, the Destroyer, the Creator, the Magician, the Ruler, the Sage and the Fool. She has even devised a questionnaire which enables people to discover which archetypes are dominant in their lives at a given moment, and which archetypes have something to do with the Shadow – that aspect of ourselves which we like least and may disown altogether.

I would disagree, however, with the view which has been expressed sometimes that every subpersonality has an archetype at its core. This is a tempting thought, but it seems to me that, because of the many origins of subpersonalities, it would be a mistake to attribute them all to archetypes. It seems to me that this diminishes the very real differences between archetypes, which are very deep and very fascinating, and much more prosaic and everyday subpersonalities, which may be far from archetypal. It would be using the word 'archetype' in an almost insulting way, just to tack it on to any subpersonality which came along; this would be to rob the word of all real meaning and contrast.

I would also disagree with the idea which I have seen expressed that subpersonalities come from our previous lives. This does not often seem to be the case.

All in all, we may say that in the archetypes we have one of the major sources of subpersonalities, and in fact some of the most interesting subpersonalities which we may come across.

GUIDED FANTASY

Some of the exercises in this book are guided fantasies. The general hints for a guided fantasy are as follows. Either get someone to read it out for you according to the instructions given, or read it out yourself in front of a tape recorder, and then play back the tape. The figures in brackets are suggested pauses in seconds: but some people are faster and some slower, so these may not be quite right for you. Amend the tape to suit the way your own mind works, if necessary.

All guided fantasies benefit from a preliminary period of relaxation. The general hints for relaxation are as follows. Lie down in a space which is comfortable, but not so comfortable that you fall asleep. Check your feet and ankles, and make sure that they are relaxed. Take a couple of deep breaths. Check your calves and knees, and make sure that they are relaxed. Take a couple of deep breaths. Check your thighs, hips and genitals, and make sure that they are relaxed. Take a couple of deep breaths. Check your tummy, your abdomen, and make sure that they are relaxed. Take a couple of deep breaths. Check your chest, and make sure that it is relaxed. Take a couple of deep breaths. Check your back, and make sure that it is relaxed. Take a couple of deep breaths. Check your hands and arms, and make sure that they are relaxed. Take a couple of deep breaths. Check your neck and shoulders, and make sure that they are relaxed. Take a couple of deep breaths. Check your face, jaw and scalp, and make sure that they are relaxed. Take a couple of deep breaths. Now check back over your whole body, and make sure you haven't tightened up any of the bits you have just relaxed. If you find any pain or tension, see if you can just sigh it out. (Sigh.) See if you can sigh it away. (Sigh.) And now you can feel your whole body lying warm and heavy. (Start fantasy immediately.)

THE BEACH AND THE BUS

This is a guided fantasy. Read it slowly to a friend, or read it into a tape recorder for your own use. Then allow 20 minutes to dictate to a friend, or into a tape recorder, the images which come. The subpersonalities which come off the bus may be isolated, or may interact with one another; just allow them to follow their own ways. Describe them and their activities in as much detail as possible. Read it back, or transcribe it, later; and make it more coherent if necessary. Much can be learned about your subpersonalities from this exercise.

You are standing on a wide beach, between the forest and the sea. You are standing on a wide beach, between the forest and the sea. (5) In the far distance you can see a bus coming towards you. In the far distance you can see a bus coming towards you. (5) And on that bus are all your sub-personalities. And on that bus are all your subpersonalities. (5) And now the bus is coming nearer, and you can begin to see it more clearly. And now the bus is coming nearer, and you can begin to see it more clearly. (5) And now you can begin to see faces through the windows. And now you can begin to see faces through the windows. (5) And now the bus is quite near, and you can see it much more clearly. And now the bus is quite near, and you can see it much more clearly. (10) And now the bus comes right up to you, and stops. And now the bus comes right up to you, and stops. (10) And now the doors open, and your subpersonalities come out one by one. And as each one comes out, you will be able to see what it looks like and what it does, and describe it. And now the doors open, and your subpersonalities come out one by one. And as each one comes out, you will be able to see what it looks like and what it does, and describe it. And the first one is coming off the bus right now. And the first one is coming off the bus right now.

Chapter 7

What are subpersonalities?

How we compartmentalize our minds

Having looked at the various ways in which we are already familiar with the idea of subpersonalities, it is time to introduce a little order into the proceedings, and ask the questions: What are subpersonalities? How do we get them? Why are they so common?

THE CONTINUUM OF DISSOCIATION

One of the easiest things for the human mind to do is to put things into compartments. It seems that to put things into compartments saves mental energy. It is as if the mind had spring doors between these compartments which we create, and as if they close of their own accord. In fact, if we want to relate the various parts of our lives in a fluid and open fashion, we have to expend quite a lot of energy in holding those spring doors open.

But the compartments of the mind may have walls which are thicker or thinner, the walls may be higher or lower, the doors may have very weak springs or very strong ones. As we shall see later, it is actually as if the springs were adjustable, so that if we have the right tools we can alter a strong and rigid spring into a weak and flexible one. In some cases we can remove doors altogether, and knock two rooms into one.

If we now translate this image into everyday terms, we can say that there is a line of degrees of compartmentalization, ranging from getting absorbed in a TV programme at one end of the line, all the way over to psychiatric states of multiple personalities at the other. The line looks like this:

ASCs–Moods–Subpersonalities–Possession–Multiple personality

This is called the continuum of dissociation, because it runs from the least dissociated states – at the beginning of the line – to the most dissociated states at the end of the line.

At one end of this line we have altered states of consciousness (ASCs). Some of these are very mild. For example, when we are watching a TV programme, and get really absorbed in it, identifying perhaps with the hero or heroine, squirming if they squirm, and so on, that is a sort of mild trance. It is a mildly altered state of consciousness. We can recognize it because if another person tries to interact with us while we are in such a state, they find it hard to do so. It is as if we had gone off somewhere else, as if we were not there in the room at all. But it only needs the programme to end, or even for the ads to come on, and we are back to normal.

Similarly with dreams. While we are having them, we are in a very different state of consciousness from our waking state. But soon after we wake up, we are back to normal. These states of consciousness are really different, but they don't last long, and we can always come back from them if we really want to. Similarly with those odd states between sleeping and waking, where some unusual things can happen.

Alcoholic states are rather similar, though here it may take time for the influence to wear off. We may not be able to be sober in an instant, as we can with the previous two states. But they do wear off before too long, and we can predict pretty well when this will happen, so there is some measure of control there.

So all these things at the left-hand end of the line are quite transient and wear off quite predictably. Then quite close to this we find moods – that is states of mind which we cannot shake off at will but which go away quite unpredictably after a while. These may be quite hard to shake off at times, and some people are much more subject to moods than others. So we cannot get rid of them just by wanting to, and they may hang around longer than intoxication or a drugged state, so they are further along the line than the previous things.

Then come subpersonalities, defined as *semi-permanent and semi-autonomous regions of the personality capable of acting as a person*; some of which seem to be universal, and which again are quite normal. We have looked at a number of these in the last few chapters. We shall be meeting many more of them later, and finding out how psychotherapy or counselling can deal with those we do not like.

Then comes possession, defined here as states of mind where we seem to be taken over by another person or other being, voluntarily or involuntarily. This happens voluntarily in some religious rituals, where the worshipper invites the god or goddess to come in. There are photographs, for example, of worshippers of the god Legbe in Haiti, which show the same positions and the same movements carried out by different people at different times, all under the influence of Legbe. But if it happens involuntarily, and some entity or being takes the person over, the person may become quite unrecognizable, have a different voice, different knowledge, and so forth, and this can be very frightening, not only for the person, but for those around him or her. This may require specialized treatment from people who are experienced in this sort of spiritual emergency, rather than ordinary psychotherapy.

And then comes multiple personality disorder, where we have no knowledge at all of at least one of the persons inside us, persons who may be leading quite a different life, and who take over quite unpredictably, causing a real psychiatric problem. Such problems can sometimes be dealt with by psychotherapy, particularly when hypnosis is used as well, but they can also be very resistant to treatment. They are often associated with sexual abuse in childhood.

The left-hand end of this continuum is quite normal and every-day, and the right-hand end is more of a psychiatric problem, which may be quite hard to treat, and which has been recounted in books like *The Three Faces of Eve*, *Sybil*, *The Minds of Billy Milligan*, *Voices*, *When Rabbit Howls*, and so forth, some of which have been made into films seen on TV.

Subpersonalities, which are mostly quite normal, cover the middle part of this scale. They can at times become a problem, and this is most likely when we hotly deny that we have any such thing. If we try to push them aside or deny their existence, this is likely to cause trouble. Subpersonalities have to be taken at times as solid characters, but they are really in process, and may split into two, or merge into one, may appear or disappear.

There are twenty-five (at least) synonyms for subpersonalities, such as ego states, subselves, subidentities, identity states, alter-personalities, deeper potentials, and so on. They are common in everyday life and are often mentioned in literature and the media generally, as we have already seen, and will see again later.

THE NATURE OF SUBPERSONALITIES

Most of us have had the experience of being 'taken over' by a part of ourselves which we didn't know was there. We say, 'I don't know what got into me.' This is generally a negative experience, although it can be positive too. The way in which we usually recognize the presence of a subpersonality is that we find ourselves, in a particular situation, acting in ways which we do not like or which go against our interests. We find ourselves unable to change this by an act of will or a conscious decision. This lasts as long as the situation lasts – perhaps a few minutes, perhaps an hour, perhaps a few hours – and then it changes by itself when we leave this situation and go into a different one.

Since this can happen in all sorts of different ways, it makes sense to say that the individual can sometimes be seen as a single self, but at other times appears to be many selves. These other selves will change somewhat as the individual shifts from situation to situation and person to person. Sometimes these other selves are on our side and help us, and sometimes they seem to be against us, criticizing us or sabotaging us.

The question as to whether there are parts of a person each with a will of its own is one which has fascinated nearly everyone who has had to work with people in any depth. Phrases like 'On the one hand I want to . . . on the other hand I don't', 'I don't know how I could have done it', 'It was as if a voice was telling me off' are so common that they inevitably give a counsellor or therapist the cue that more than one system is at work. Internalized mothers and fathers are so common that it has almost become a joke. All these are examples of ways in which the idea of subpersonalities presents itself very patently and obviously.

EXAMPLE

I heard an old woman once talking about herself in a programme about dreams, and this is what she said:

I could give you a whole list of the persons I can be. I am an old peasant woman who thinks of cooking and of the house. I am a scholar who thinks about deciphering manuscripts. I am a psychotherapist who thinks about how to interpret people's dreams. I am a mischievous little boy who enjoys the company of a ten-year-old and playing mischievous tricks on adults, and so on. I could give you twenty more such characters. They suddenly enter you, but if you see what is happening you can keep them out of your system, play with them and put them aside again. But if you are possessed, they enter you involuntarily and you act them out involuntarily.

It is clear from this that on the one hand it does make sense to take subpersonalities as solid objects, as it were. But at the same time we must remember that we are not talking about things like chairs and tables. We are talking about processes which are actually very fluid and in change, and may be much bigger than we understand at first.

On the one hand it will be very useful for us to think in terms of little people within the person. But on the other hand we must beware of giving them a status which they do not deserve and which would not be proper. They are in fact moments in a process of change and development which is lifelong.

A WARNING

There is one warning which should be given here, however, and that is that I do not believe that subpersonalities should be taken as taking away the responsibility of the social person.

There have been attempts to say that if the idea of subpersonalities holds water, then it could be said that if one subpersonality committed a crime, then another subpersonality could not be held responsible. This has actually been tried.

John Watkins is a hypnotherapist with a great interest in subpersonalities, which he calls ego states. He is often used as an expert in legal cases where there is a defence of diminished responsibility due to the presence of a 'second personality' or something of that kind. In each case the defence lawyers tried to argue that the person in the dock was in effect not the person who had committed the crime – even if they happened to share the same physical body. And in each case Watkins argued that there

A LIST OF WANTS

Draw up a list of all the things you want. This should include things you have now and want to keep on having. They can be concrete things, abstract qualities, anything at all. For example, they might include money, health, love, success, power, enlightenment, a new car, a diamond, whatever. Ignore this list, and write your own list, using as many words as you want for each thing. No need to judge it, just write it.

When you have got about twenty wants, look over the list and pick out the four to nine items which seem most important to you. While you are doing this, you could group two or more of the items if they seem to be more or less saying the same thing. Or you could split one into two if that made more sense. This is just for you alone, so try not to compare your list with what someone else might write.

Now draw two concentric circles, the outer one as big as you can make it, and the inner one quite small. The inner one represents your real self, the part of you that is not a subpersonality at all. Divide up the outer part into four to nine segments, each segment for one of the four to nine wants which you have identified as most important. In each segment, draw or paint a symbol to represent one of the four to nine wants. When you have finished your drawing or painting, look at what you have done and imagine that each segment represents one of your subpersonalities. See if you can give a name to each of these subpersonalities. Find a name which means something to you, no matter how conventional or unconventional it may be. It could be one word or it could be a whole phrase – there could even be two or more names if you can't make up your mind.

Finally, look over the whole thing and see how it compares with other exercises you have done. Is there an overlap, and if so what does this tell you? How do these subpersonalities relate to one another? See what you can learn from the whole experience.

were in effect two different personalities involved, one guilty and one innocent; and the one in the dock was the innocent one. There would be no way of punishing the guilty one without, by the same token and at the same time, punishing the innocent one. But in each case the court refused to accept this argument.

There is of course an important difference between subpersonalities and multiple personality. There are much higher barriers and divisions present in the latter. They have quite different positions on the line we drew earlier. But even in cases of true multiple personality, it seems to me that it would be wrong to diminish the responsibility of the social person who is visible to all. There is just one legal person who signs cheques, owns property, enters into contracts, and so forth. In that sense the courts were right.

So the warning is: don't run away with the idea that the concept of subpersonalities can be used to diminish any of our human responsibilities for all of our actions, no matter how partial or one-sided or inadequate the impulse behind it may be.

(1) 'I treat people as equals. If they seem to be putting themselves down, this brings them up. If they seem to be putting on
airs, it brings them down to the level.' Is this what you do?

Wish I could do that	0
Perhaps occasionally I can	1
Yes, quite often I do	2
Yes, all the time	3

(2) 'Power and control are good when applied to things, but they
are not good in relation to people.' Do you agree?

No, people need and like to be controlled	0
I think there has to be some power and control exercised	1
I like to play down power and control in my dealings with people	2
Yes, I agree totally	3

(3) 'There is nothing we can give each other which is better than
the truth.' Do you agree?

No, there has to be some colour and imagination in the world	0
The truth is not always the best thing	1
I am inclined to believe it	2
Yes, I agree	3

(4) If someone asks you for directions will you tell them the way,
even if you don't know for sure?

Every time	0
Quite often, yes	1
Very rarely, I might	2
No	3

(5) If you say you will do something, do you keep your word?

Yes, unless something more exciting comes up	0
Yes, unless there is a good reason not to	1
Yes, unless something unforeseen prevents me	2
Yes	3

How to score

This is to discover whether you have an Adult subpersonality.

0–5   You do not have much in the way of an Adult at all, and
       this may make you rather hard to relate to. Why not try to

cultive your Adult a bit more? Everyone around you would benefit from this, and you too.

6–10   You do have an Adult, and it is in a modest position, not too suppressed. Cultivate it wisely.

11–15   You do have an Adult subpersonality, and it is very well developed. Just watch out that it does not take over too much, in an exclusive way.

Chapter 8

Altered states of consciousness
Something we are all familiar with

This may be a good place to discuss the idea of altered states of consciousness. It was apparently the custom of the ancient Teutons to make any important decision twice, once drunk and once sober. They thus got the benefit of two different angles on the problem. This suggests a regular and dependable contrast between the two states of consciousness.

Almost everyone has at least two altered states of consciousness – the dreaming state and the state between waking and sleeping.

This latter is called hypnagogia. It is a state in which it is particularly easy to get in touch with extra-sensory perception. This includes such things as mediumship, telepathy, clairvoyance and out-of-body experiences. It is as if this waking–sleeping state opened up the possibility of getting in touch with a psychic subpersonality.

Now it has often been pointed out that much of what comes out in these circumstances (spirit messages, etc.) is quite trivial and not very impressive. But if, as I am suggesting, what is involved here is communication from one system to another, from one subpersonality to another, this is easier to understand. The apparent triviality, tangentiality and superficiality of much of that which comes from the paranormal may be due to the data having to be laboriously translated from one system to another.

In addition, many of us have experienced alcoholic intoxication, marijuana intoxication and other drug states. Most of us know that when we have been drinking things look different. People look more attractive and sound more interesting, we are more inclined to take risks, our moods switch more easily, and so forth. Less common, but still quite frequent experiences are those

of meditation, so-called spirit possession and hypnotic states. Scientists studying meditation and similar topics may have to go into an altered state of consciousness themselves in order to do the work adequately. This gives us the notion of a state-specific science. We would now call this science which involves getting into a specific subpersonality. For example, a scientist studying the effects of LSD would have to take LSD in order to have any understanding at all of the issues involved.

EXAMPLE

Let us take an example from the world of fiction, which some readers will have experienced. In the Charlie Chaplin film *City Lights*, Charlie is befriended by a drunken millionaire, who takes him home and gives him the run of the house. In the morning, the millionaire wakes up, sees this dirty tramp spoiling his nice house, and kicks him out. Quite bemused, Charlie mooches off back to his usual haunts. That evening the millionaire is drunk again, sees Charlie, recognizes him as his pal, and takes him back again. In the morning, sober again, he rejects him again, and so on. In other words, there are two personalities involved here: the drunken millionaire, who treats Charlie in one way, and the sober millionaire who treats him quite differently. In one state of consciousness Charlie is a friend, in the other he is a nuisance. These repeated states of consciousness, with their consistency over time, certainly approach our definition of subpersonalities.

What we have seen so far in this chapter is that we are talking about things which are in the experience of many, perhaps most of us. We are not talking about anything which is hard to understand. And it is something which we can explore quite deliberately and intentionally.

ANIMAL IN A CAGE

This is a brief guided fantasy. Check with the general instructions for guided fantasy to be found on p. 76.

You are an animal in a cage. Notice what animal you are, and check all the details of size, age, sex, and so forth.

If you could say something to the cage, what would you say?

Now be the cage. As the cage, what do you reply to the animal?

Go back and forth with this dialogue for a while.

After a while, you notice, as the animal, that the door of the cage is open. What happens next?

Open your eyes when this is all over, and write down what happened, paying attention to all the fine details. Look back over what you have written, and see what you can learn from it about your life.

Chapter 9

Maturity

Connections to the world outside us

One of the ways we can go wrong in this work is to lay all the stress on what is inside the person. We are intimately connected with the world around us in a million ways. We swim in a community of souls, an ocean of impressions, a universe of events. All our inner problems are reflected in the outer world, and all the problems of the world are reflected in our inner psyche.

One of the bad things which psychology can do is to psychologize all problems, so that instead of dealing with the world we deal with our inner selves. It is the 'instead of' which is harmful. So we have to pay attention to that connection, and make sure that we do not set it aside as of no importance. In order to explore it, we may again try an exercise, this time one of quite a different type.

It is quite scary to see the way in which these conflicts reflect back and forth inside us and outside us, and it brings home to us just how much the inner world and the outer world depend on each other and even constitute each other.

One of the most useful things the concept of subpersonalities can do for us is to make us realize how the way we treat people around us and how we treat the people inside us is very similar. Recent research by Linda Ford in the USA has shown that this can be demonstrated in group work – we may actually project on to members of the groups we work with the subpersonalities we do not wish to acknowledge inside us. The ways we treat our inner enemies may be very close to the ways in which we treat our enemies out there in the world. A marvellous woman called Joanna Macy has been going round the world running workshops where this is recognized and dealt with.

INNER AND OUTER CONFLICT

A pack of Tarot cards is usually used for this exercise – one of those where each card has a different scene. The Mother-peace pack is particularly suitable, because it has more varied people and objects in each scene than any other. But any pictures can be used – art postcards, pictures cut out of magazines, anything at all which strikes the imagination.

This is an exercise which emerged directly out of the experience of the BAC Working Party on Counselling and Peace. It tries to link the conflicts we have inside ourselves to the real conflicts so visible out there in the world. And it uses a basically transpersonal approach, which brings in paradox and reversal.

1. Lay out the cards so that you can see them all clearly. Look at all the cards laid out, and see if you can let two of them stand out for you. One which you like, which speaks to you in a positive way, and one which you dislike, which speaks to you in a negative way. Just spend some time choosing which two to pick, and then pick them up and hold them.

Now looking at your two cards, see if they link with an inner conflict; something problematic for you, something where you wrestle with yourself, or do battle with yourself. It will have two sides to it. Two energies, two forces, two inclinations, two motivations, two aspects. The whole thing depends on the idea of conflict between two sides. If you have a choice between a more dramatic and a less dramatic conflict, please choose the more dramatic one.

Sit down with a sheet of paper and a pen. Divide the paper into two, and write on one side the one side of the conflict, and on the other, the other, making clear which card represents which side of the conflict, and why. Write down the way in which each thing in the picture fits in with one side of the conflict. Give each side a title.

2. Now look at your Tarot cards again and see how they could stand for an *external* conflict – one that is important or revealing in some way – between people in the world. Don't make this into an intellectual task, just let your intuition light on the first thing which comes to mind. Don't let this take more than 30 seconds at most, and see if you can let it be quite immediate. Here too it may be that one card is

positive and the other negative. Write those on the same sheet of paper, or on a different one also divided into two, if there is no room on the first one.

3. Now we are going to go back to the first conflict, the *internal* one. What you do now is to explore the idea that the card which showed one side actually stands for the other side, and the one which stood for the second side actually stands for the first side, in terms of the real situation. So take another sheet of paper, divide it into two in the way you did before, but this time put down all the ways in which the picture on the one card fits with the *other* side of the conflict, and vice versa. Start with your own original associations with the various bits of the scene, but then feel free to go on to add further insights. This may seem hard or even impossible at first, or you may object to doing it for one reason or another. If so, just put it aside for the moment, and perhaps you may feel differently later, when you have had time to get used to the idea. I said that we would be using paradox in this exercise, and you have now experienced what that means.

4. And now we do the same thing with the external conflict. Use your cards to show how the good card is actually the bad one, and the bad card is actually the good one, in terms of the real situation out there in the world. You don't have to use words like 'good' and 'bad' if you don't want to. Again use a different sheet of paper to help clarify the matter. Start with your own original associations with the various bits of the scene, but then feel free to go on to add further insights.

5. The final step is to use your cards to discover how the conflicts can be resolved: first, the inner one, and then, if possible, the outer one. Here you forget about good and bad cards, and just use both your cards in any way that seems useful.

Now just spend a minute or two reflecting on that exercise, anything at all that struck you at any point about what happened. You might want to write down any insights which seem useful to you.

Chapter 10

Relationships
How to understand what is going on

Recognizing subpersonalities is also very useful in our inter-
actions with other people. For example, when we criticize
someone, they very often find it hard to take, because they take it
personally. But once we think and speak in terms of subpersonalities, the process is much easier. 'I think your Martyr is
trying to make me feel guilty. Do you agree?' We have stopped
saying that the whole person is at fault. Now we are drawing
attention to a problem for us. And we are putting it in a way that
shows that it may also be a problem for the person themselves. It
is more straight and more accurate to speak in this way.

We are responsible for our subpersonalities, just as we are
responsible for our children, our pets and our car. We certainly
need to see that they don't cause trouble to ourselves or to others.
But *we are not them*. People can use the concept of subpersonalities
very effectively. And this is true most of all when they're dealing
with problems in interpersonal relationships.

In a couple, for example, if I say, 'I am jealous', it describes the
whole of me, and I am overwhelmed by it. It may go against all
my values. The completeness of the statement may even make me
feel contemptuous of myself. It is hard to admit it, when I feel that
this describes the totality of who I am. But if I respect the plurality
in myself, the whole feeling changes. I no longer see my jealous
self (The Jealous One) as the whole of me. And then I have gained
the distance I need to observe it, listen to it, and let it teach me
something. In this way I come into possession of more of myself
and extend my own inner kingdom.

This seems extremely useful as a general strategy, and it gives
a much better handle by which to grasp many social situations. If
I can say, 'Yes, part of me does feel that, but only part of me', that

does justice to the fact that I do feel it, but does not overwhelm me by suggesting that that is *all* that I feel.

CLARIFYING MEETINGS

Have a set of clarifying meetings, to get to know each of your subpersonalities better. Bring on each in turn, and ask questions of each one in turn. Record the answers in some way for the best results. Use any of the questions we have mentioned so far, and add any other questions you may think of.

Another way in which we can use the idea is to see that certain tangles are all too easy to set up. For example, what happens if Joe has an internal Punitive Father and Guilty Son, and his partner Eve has an internal Victim Daughter and Punitive Mother?

When the Punitive Father belonging to Joe comes on the scene, shouting and complaining, the Victim Daughter is brought out in Eve. So now Eve feels victimized. She suffers and feels oppressed, she feels put down and hard done by.

At another time, when the Punitive Mother belonging to Eve comes on the scene, criticizing and nagging, the Guilty Son emerges into the light. So now Joe feels guilty. He feels as if he can never get anything right in her eyes, and that he is less than a man.

Each is afraid of the other, and afraid of appearing weak: but the only way of not appearing weak is to put the other partner down, in a power struggle which neither can enjoy or understand. This sort of pattern happens in many relationships, and the idea of subpersonalities can be very helpful in sorting out exactly what is going on.

In a lesbian relationship, Ursula had an internal Nurturing Mother and Compliant Daughter: her partner Alison had an internal Vulnerable Child and Controlling Mother. When Alison's Vulnerable Child came on the scene, the Nurturing Mother of Ursula came out and joined her, and Alison felt taken care of and secure; but when Ursula's Nurturing Mother got tired, and retired into the background again, her Compliant Daughter came on the scene. At this point, Alison's Controlling Mother came forward and joined her, and Ursula felt bossed about and unhappy.

We can avoid a lot of problems if we can be aware of what our subpersonalities are up to in a relationship. Which ones of ours bring out which ones in the other person, and vice versa. And this is very important if we want to have peace of mind.

A MEETING ROUND THE TABLE

Use one of the methods above to identify some of your subpersonalities. Then have a meeting between them, all sitting round a table in your imagination. Prepare an agenda before the meeting, so that you know in advance what the issues are which you want to get resolved. Appoint a Conflict Manager: for this you can choose an old subpersonality you trust, or create a new one. Then start negotiating. Use a tape recorder or write down the answers you get, so as to have a record of the meeting. Important discoveries about yourself can be made in this way.

Chapter 11

Dream characters
Making use of our dreams

The characters who appear in our dreams are of the nature of subpersonalities within us. We create them, and they perform on our stage. Sometimes the importance of these dream characters is more obvious to other people than it is to us ourselves. For example, one man had several dreams in which a character came up who was always postponing things and then doing them very slowly and with great difficulty. He began to call this character 'Slowcoach', and talked about it with his wife. And now whenever his wife finds her husband procrastinating over a decision, she asks, 'Is it really a difficult decision requiring lots of thought, or is it old "Slowcoach" up to his tricks again?' And this often seems to clarify the matter in a useful way.

A woman called Ann had dreams about a 'Ray of White Light' which always kept telling her to be more independent, not to need other people, and so forth. Again she talked to her partner about it, and soon, when she refused help with some task or criticized people for not standing on their own two feet, she got asked, 'Is that Ann or the "Ray of White Light" talking?' – a question which she found very useful, as she then looked at her real feelings about the matter.

Dreams are a very important source of information about ourselves. If you can, keep a dream book, where you write down all your dreams. There is a proverb which says: 'An uninterpreted dream is like an unopened letter.' Most of us can remember our dreams if we set ourselves to do so. And it can be very valuable to work on them with someone else, or with a group. Dream-sharing is a group activity which can be very enriching.

It is good to watch for the names of your dream characters. Sometimes the dream itself gives the person a name. If not, you

A DREAM CHARACTER

TWO DREAM
CHARACTERS

can invent a name that seems to capture the person's character. Or you can use a descriptive name. If it is a masculine figure, it may be Brave Warrior, Wise Elder, Old Miser, Sneaky Crook, Juvenile Delinquent, Young Prince, Trickster, Tribal Brother. If this is a feminine figure you may find yourself calling her Wise Mother, Tyrant Mother, Earth Mother, Faithful Sister, My Lady Soul, Lady of the Sparkling Eyes. If she fits the mythical role, you may give her a mythical name: Helen, Iseult of the White Hands, Guinevere.

A child may be very important, as we saw earlier, and there may be various types of inner child we could get in touch with in dreams, as we saw in Chapter 4.

Once a subpersonality has been named, it becomes easier to use it in this kind of way, as a method of raising awareness of what is going on internally.

It is important to realize that not only the people in a dream, but also the objects, may represent subpersonalities. A house very often represents the whole personality. An animal may represent a very much alive part of ourselves. The sea may sometimes represent the unconscious mind. Even a wall may turn out to represent some part of our personality, as we saw in Chapter 5.

Not everyone finds it easy to remember their dreams, but it is something which can be developed with practice. After all, research has shown that everyone has about five dreams every night. So this is something which can be cultivated, if the right approach is used. Some hints which people have found useful are:

1 On going to sleep, imagine your mind as an empty TV screen, waiting for a programme to be projected on to it.
2 Suggest to yourself that you are going to have at least one dream and remember it.
3 Don't open your eyes straight away when you wake up, but let the dream images come back, and go over them.
4 When you feel that this recall is complete, move to another position in which you normally sleep, and more images may come back.
5 Have a paper and pencil handy, and jot down what you can remember straight away. Some people like to use cassette recorders instead of pen and paper.
6 Be sure not to miss out any unusual scenes and any words,

particularly unfamiliar words or phrases, which might have come from a dream. These can be particularly important and revealing.

7 It is better not to open your eyes, and it is possible to learn to write with your eyes closed. Some people have even bought boards with wires across, as used by blind people, to make sure they write in straight lines.

8 Record dreams in the order in which you recall them. Don't try to work out which came first in the night.

If these hints are followed, there is no reason why anyone at all should not be able to remember and use their dreams for help and guidance, and particularly for the evocation of subpersonalities.

DREAM DRAWING AND DIALOGUE

Have some felt pens or coloured pencils ready. Bring to mind a recent or significant dream. A recurring dream is particularly good for this. Tell the dream out loud, in the present tense, as if it were happening now, and make it as detailed as possible.

At the end of the dream, open your eyes, take the colours and draw your dream quickly, not worrying about whether you are doing it well or badly. Make sure that there is at least one person or object which is explicitly drawn out in a fairly realistic way. Don't spend too much time on this: the object is not to show the drawing, but to use it.

Now pick out one person or object from what you have drawn, and talk to it. Put it on a chair or cushion and imagine that it can hear you talking to it. Perhaps you want to ask it a question, or perhaps you want to tell it what you think about it, or perhaps you want to tell it to do something, or stop doing something – whatever comes naturally and easily.

Now go over and take its place (just put the paper aside so that you do not spoil it), and talk back to yourself, as if you now were this person or object. Go back and forth with this dialogue until some satisfactory ending is reached.

Chapter 12

Books and films: *Steppenwolf*
Subpersonalities in action on the stage

It was not until the eighteenth century that the idea of the unconscious really caught on and started to be understood. This was the first essential step. Until the division is made between conscious and unconscious, there is no place, as it were, for the subpersonalities to be.

At first the fascination was with dual personalities. One person could have an alter ego who shadowed him. But as the nineteenth century went on, the emphasis changed more towards multiplicity. The whole area of the novel, which began about this time, is of course very much open to subpersonalities. The novelist has this power of developing latent subpersonalities in herself or himself, and of transforming them into literary characters.

Anyone keeping a personal diary tends to develop a dual personality. A second personality starts to emerge. And then a peculiar interpersonal relationship develops between the diarist and the fictitious second self. This second self may then at a given point come to life, so to speak, in the form of a literary character in whom the writer will bring out his secret problems.

Of course, things are not always this subtle. The media have always been prone to using the more dramatic dual or multiple personality, which are clearly pathological states. Who has not heard of Jekyll and Hyde? There is a powerful image here, which has made such an impression on the public mind that one can refer to it with all kinds of people and be understood. Yet there a drug was involved. It was one of those magic drugs, to be sure, which are common in literature. The drug is a literary device to help us to go along with the story. And we

may feel immune from such things because no such drug has been given to us. Our own inner conflicts are not as strong or as serious as this. So we can dismiss the idea.

Similarly, in *The Moonstone*, by Wilkie Collins. In this book the whole plot depends on the way in which a man behaves quite differently, but consistently so, when under the influence of a drug – in this case laudanum.

The work of Dostoevsky shows us how powerful the idea of subpersonalities can be, when in *The Brothers Karamazov* the conflict between the good self and the evil self in Ivan Karamazov is brought out with stunning effect.

STEPPENWOLF

But the best example for our purpose here is the novel *Steppenwolf*, where Hermann Hesse takes time off from his main narrative to write a complete *Treatise on the Steppenwolf*, and this was published separately in 1975 with some remarkable paintings by Jaroslav Bradac, based on his work for the film of *Steppenwolf*, which came out in 1975, directed by Fred Haines. In this treatise, Hesse explains that his hero Harry Haller, as well as being a human being, was also a wolf of the steppes. What we are really talking about here is a wolf-like subpersonality.

Hesse is here playing with the idea that perhaps the wolf is a defence, a result of some events in childhood which have resulted in this way of dealing with the world. (We saw in Chapter 4 that such things do happen, in fact.) He goes on to say that perhaps such internal animals are not uncommon, and that sometimes they may be benign rather than a constant problem. But for Harry Haller the man and the wolf did not go the same way together. They did not help each other, but were in continual and deadly enmity. The one existed simply and solely to harm the other.

So far we are on rather similar ground to the other literary examples we have quoted, where for the most part the internal characters appear to be malevolent and dangerous. Hesse goes on to say that when one did any action in the world, the other would criticize and laugh, or criticize and weep, and see through it. Any good action would be weakened and its enjoyment lost; any bad action would be wished away before it could be savoured. We shall see in a later chapter how common are these internal critics and saboteurs, and how they are dealt with in therapy.

But now Hesse becomes rather more sophisticated than the other writers we have mentioned so far: he says that the Steppenwolf Harry is still better off than the bourgeois who has no such conflict, but keeps to the middle way all the time. He does at least have some conception of the heights and the depths, the extremes of life. And he does have a sense of humour. But the only way really to make all this work for him instead of against him is to know himself better.

But then Hesse makes his masterstroke. He shows how this story of a man and a wolf is a convenient fiction. It is a way of simplifying and making understandable what in reality is far from simple and not at all understandable. For in reality there is not a single human being, not the simplest or most primitive, who is so obvious as to be explained as the sum of two or three principal elements. Harry, he says, consists of a hundred or a thousand selves, not of two. His life oscillates, as everyone's does, not merely between two poles, such as the body and the spirit, the saint and the sinner, but between thousands, between innumerable poles.

People generally, says Hesse, are not capable of thought in any high degree. Even the most cultivated of them use absurd simplifications in their thought and understanding. People will do anything to make their life easier. And the idea that there is just one simple, single self is the crudest and most oversimplified assumption of all.

Hesse goes on to say that in a drama or a novel it is the whole cast of characters which represent a single human soul, not any one of them. When Faust says, 'Two souls, alas, dwell in my breast!' he has forgotten Mephisto and a whole crowd of other souls that he also has in his breast. The trouble with Harry is that he thinks that two is too many – in reality the problem is much more that two are not enough. Two can tear you apart; many can enrich and sustain you. This again links with the argument which we shall try to maintain in later chapters.

This is a very fine and sophisticated view of subpersonalities, and we can go along with most of it. The man knows about the wolf, and the wolf knows about the man, and there is no cut-off or hiding at all. This is the normal state with subpersonalities – they are or can be perfectly well aware of one another, though sometimes they may not care about one another enough to bother.

So with those misunderstandings out of the way, we can go along with Hesse's ideas pretty well intact. It is important not to dismiss this as mere fiction. A therapist once told me that he once asked a patient to imagine a person other than himself if he were to look in a mirror. He answered that he saw a werewolf. As he continued, he realized the meaning of what he imagined seeing: the werewolf was the despised image that he didn't want the world to know about.

Subpersonalities, in a word, are real, are important, and are well within the range of normality. To recognize them is a sign of maturity, and to deal with them a sign of mental health.

TWELVE ANIMALS

Lie flat on your back, relax and breathe easily. Now choose out of the following creatures one that interests you: ram, bull, bird, crab, lion, bear, snake, scorpion, centaur, goat, monkey, fish. Pick the first one that your mind alights on, and stay with it. Picture that creature. Notice how it moves. Notice its surroundings.

Now slowly get up, and keeping your eyes closed, start to move like that creature. Imagine yourself in its surroundings. Get a feel of that creature in your body, and of its movements. Let your body move in such a way as to reflect in some way your sense of being that creature. As you get into the movements, notice what feelings or images come to you. Stay in character for at least three minutes.

Afterwards, notice how you felt about the creature. Is there a part of you which resembles this creature? How do you feel about that part of you?

Write down any insights which come to you after this exercise.

Chapter 13

Let's look at some of the explanations
Freud and psychoanalysis

Let us now look at how the idea of subpersonalities has been used in psychotherapy and counselling. Over the years, psychotherapists and counsellors have found ways of handling and dealing with troublesome subpersonalities. Some of these ways are adaptable to use by anyone, and many of our exercises in this book are based on them.

In the next few chapters, we shall examine the main methods of psychotherapy which are now available. Each of these methods has its own traditions, its own ways of using the ideas, and so each of them has something unique to contribute.

Perhaps the idea of subpersonalities may be a way of enabling one therapy to talk to another. If we want to get the benefit of all the discoveries of the past thirty years, we have to take some risks. We have to try new things, and just because the idea of subpersonalities does not come from any one school, it can perhaps be useful. I have come across no less then twenty-five different names for subpersonalities in the literature. Perhaps it can at the very least act as a kind of Rosetta Stone, enabling translations to be made between one discipline and another. This would certainly be my hope.

The story really starts back in the eighteenth century, as we shall see in Chapter 22, but we shall pick it up at the turn of the century, when Freud came on to the map, because he is the first name which most of us have heard of.

Freud really said very little about subpersonalities. It is true he did talk about the blind, energetic, pleasure-seeking id; the priggish and punitive superego; the ego, battling for its being by diverting the energy of others to its own use. The drama of the way in which these three characters interact has an economy and a terseness. The ego develops defence mechanisms for dealing with the threat of id impulses; repression, rationalization, denial, projection, and the rest. Balances are struck between the actors, and in the balance is character and neurosis. But Freud himself never said much about how to use all this actually in the therapy session, and his followers have mostly followed suit.

In the 1940s Melanie Klein started talking about internal objects as being very important to the understanding of infantile fantasies. And this led on to the distinction which the object relations school developed between the real or true self, and the false self or selves. It is a curious fact, however, that none of these psychoanalysts developed any way of working with the subpersonalities they had discovered. It was left to others to take the ideas further and make them usable.

STATUE

This is a guided fantasy. Refer to the instructions on p. 76.

Now I want you to imagine that you are in a very dark building. You can't see anything at all yet, but you know that it is some kind of art museum or art gallery for sculpture. Directly in front of you, there is a statue or sculpture of yourself as you really are. It might be realistic or abstract, but this statue somehow expresses your basic existence. Look into the darkness, and as the light gradually increases you will be able to see what this statue is like.

Slowly the light will increase, and you will be able to discover more about this statue. What is its shape and form? How large is it, and what is it made of? As you are able to see it more clearly, discover still more details. Walk around it and look at it from different angles. Go close to it and touch it with your hands. How does it feel?

Now I want you to become this statue. Imagine that you are this statue, and change your posture and position to fit the form of the statue. How do you feel as this statue? What are you like? Describe yourself as this statue, 'I am . . . '. What is your existence like as this statue? What happens to you, and how do you feel about this?

Now bring this statue to life in your imagination. As a living statue, what do you do and what is your life like? Take a little time to discover more about your existence as this living statue.

Now become yourself again and look at this statue. Does the statue seem any different to you now? Has anything changed? How do you feel now towards this statue? Slowly get ready to say goodbye to this statue.

Say goodbye now, return to your existence in this room, and quietly absorb what you have just experienced. Write down anything which you think is worth remembering about this.

In psychoanalytic terms this is an exercise about the ego-ideal. But as we shall see later on this is not the only way of regarding it.

Chapter 14

How do we work with our subpersonalities?

The Jungian tradition and active imagination

Jung, on the other hand, had a lot more to say about it. Some of his first work, in the first ten years of this century, was with association tests. This is an interesting scientific test, where the experimenter says a word and the subject comes back with the first word which comes into his or her head.

Through the use of this device, Jung became convinced that within the person there were distinct regions. Each of these had a life of its own. They were not completely separate from one another or from the central ego. He described them as semi-autonomous, to indicate that they were partly independent, but not wholly so. He also called them the feeling-toned complexes. His first thought was that the complex was like a theme in music, which came back in various forms in different circumstances, but later he saw it more as a subpersonality.

Jung's subpersonalities included archetypes (as we saw in Chapter 6), such as the Ego, the Persona, the Shadow, the Anima, the Wise Old Man, the Wise Old Woman, the Self, etc., as well as the complexes, such as the Mother complex and the Father complex. Each of these could behave as an organizing centre, and each could take charge in turn of the feelings of 'I' and of behaviour. They all have an innate basis and yet all are influenced by experience. They all grow and change through experience.

Jung went further. And this is a strand of his work which has been taken up very much in recent years by followers such as James Hillman and Mary Watkins. Not only are complexes a result of problems (usually traumatic, in Jung's opinion) and a cause of problems (such as lack of control over one's daily actions), they can also be an important and healthy feature of the total person. In other words, the job of the psychotherapist is not

WISE OLD MAN

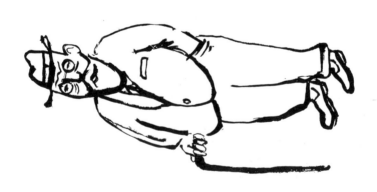

WISE OLD WOMAN

just to get rid of complexes or tinker with complexes, but also to respect, and encourage the client to respect, those complexes.

If we take this as our basis we can do all sorts of good work in psychotherapy. All we have to do is to allow and encourage these parts to speak their minds. Then they can interact with each other. And this enables them to change, merge, separate, integrate and differentiate, to transform. And to do all this the first step is to personify the complex. That is, we assume that we are talking to a person, and go ahead and do it. If we do this we may find out that these parts of ourselves are more important than we thought at first. This discovery can turn the ego into something much more minor and less dominant. We can now see the ego not as the whole psyche, but as only one member of a commune.

The members of this commune may have names, and in previous chapters we have looked at many such names. This process of naming is very important.

Another Jungian who, like Hillman, has paid attention to this matter, is Robert Johnson. But whereas Hillman says nothing about how to go about working with the subpersonalities, Johnson does. He, too, thinks it very important to name the persons who emerge as subpersonalities. This is particularly the case, of course, if the same person can be identified in several dreams, visions or other aspects of what Jung calls 'active imagination'.

ACTIVE IMAGINATION

In active imagination we fix upon a particular image, and then allow a fantasy to develop in which it becomes in some way a person. Thereafter the images have a life of their own and develop according to their own logic. This method enables conversations to take place with contents of the unconscious now personified. It does not matter how the image may come, but the essential thing is to hold on to it and not let it go until it has revealed its message through dialogue.

Jung emphasizes over and over again the distinction between passive imagination, where we merely experience a scene as if looking at it on a screen, and active imagination, where we go back and forth between the personified image and ourselves. A good way to connect to the inner parts of yourself is to think of each dream figure as an actual person living inside you. Think of each person in your dream as one of the autonomous personalities that coexist within your psyche and combine to make up your total self.

So what one has to do is to carry on a dialogue with the image which has been produced spontaneously. Of course there is no one but oneself to play the other role. So it becomes a question of going back and forth between the two or more roles.

One can usually tell whether a person is doing real active imagination by the feeling responses that come out. If the normal human reaction to the situation in the imagination would be anger, fear or intense joy, this is what the person doing active imagination should be feeling. If none of these feelings are present, then we can tell that the person is detached from the proceedings. If the feelings are not felt, the person must be just watching from a distance, not really participating, not taking it seriously. We must participate completely. We must not stray from the zone of participation into the zone of control. In active imagination we cannot exert control over the inner persons or over what is happening. We have to let the imagination flow where it will. We must always let the experience develop without trying to determine in advance what is going to happen. We must not decide in advance what is going to be said, what is going to be done.

The point is that one must be willing to engage in real dialogue with the subpersonality. It is not a question of what we would like to be the case, but of what actually is the case. We have to be genuinely open and listening. This is sometimes not easy, but if we try to ignore or dispose of parts of ourselves, only trouble can result. In physics it is said that energy can neither be created nor destroyed, and in psychology it seems to be true that subpersonalities cannot just be wished away.

TALKING TO YOUR SOUL

Write a dialogue between you and your soul, or between you and one of your other subpersonalities. Take some time to choose the right one, the subpersonality which you really need to talk to right now. Then start writing. You will find it is easier than you think. But see if you can really surrender to the process. See if you can allow your other self a real voice, not controlling it, but letting it speak. Give it the time and trouble to really learn something from it.

The Goddess Athena

In Ancient Greece there was an understanding that one was required to worship all the gods and goddesses. You might have your favourites, but none of the remaining deities could be ignored. The god or goddess whom you ignored became the one who turned against you and destroyed you. So it was with the Trojan war, in ancient Greek mythology. So it is with consciousness work. The parts of ourselves that we disown may turn against us.

This is a useful and important insight. And indeed the idea that we might have within us the god or goddess does sometimes make sense, such as when encouraging women to see strong aspects of themselves as female rather than male. Jean Shinoda Bolen, another Jungian, suggests that Athena, for example, is very warlike and very intellectual but also totally female. So this goddess can be an inspiration to women who want to enter the male world.

But what kind of reality are we talking about here? Is all this something which is way outside anything practical or real? I would suggest that these imaginal dialogues do not merely reflect or distort reality, but create reality. The real is not necessarily opposed to the imaginal, but can actually include the imaginal. Personifying is not something primitive, but something advanced and sophisticated. It tells us something about the dramatic and poetic nature of the mind. Symbolizing does not merely reflect or communicate what is already known, but is formative, and creates meaning. So the activity we are engaging in when we have a dialogue with our internal subpersonalities is a healthy and constructive one. We would not judge a play or novel with one character as necessarily better or worse than another with several characters.

After all, in the literature on personality development it is generally recognized that complexity and the recognition of different sides of the personality side by side with one another is a sign of maturity, of high development. For us to see a person as all good or all bad is regarded as less mature than to see them as partly good and partly bad, and so on. Why not apply the same reasoning to ourselves? I remember one woman client of mine who said in a puzzled voice, 'What I can't understand is how I take myself apart into all these pieces in here, and yet when I go out I feel more whole!'

So this Jungian work is very rich, and has grown over a period of fifty years or so into something which is very sophisticated and well worked out.

Chapter 15

How do we encounter our subpersonalities?
Psychodrama

Another candidate for the first use of subpersonalities in therapy is Jacob Moreno, the inventor of psychodrama. He never used the term, but he did use the approach, very freely and individually. Psychodrama is usually involved with scenes between people, and carried out in groups. There is, however, such a thing as intra-psychic psychodrama – in other words psychodrama where the characters are internal rather than external. For example, one person might have a struggle between two parts of him- or herself called Fear and Caring, which could get into a dialogue, the results of which could be very important for him or her.

Zerka Moreno talks about the multiple double technique, used in a group, where the person is on the stage with several doubles of himself or herself. Each portrays part of the person. One helper in the group acts as the person is now, while the person concerned acts as he or she was as a child; another helper acts as the person was soon after a parent's death; another helper how the person may be thirty years hence. In this way all sorts of tangles can be sorted out, as the person takes one role after another and sees things from different points of view.

Let us look at one example in some detail, where the person was working with me on a one-to-one basis. Emily felt angry with her husband. But she didn't approve of anger. So she never admitted she was angry. The anger went on working inside, just under the surface. She wanted to hit her husband sometimes. But she felt it was too dangerous to do that, and besides, she wasn't that kind of person. The desire to hit him went on working inside, just under the surface. One day she had a twinge in her shoulder. There was something about it (she saw later) that reminded her of her anger – it had the same fiery quality. There was something about it (she realized afterwards) that reminded her of hitting – it got worse when she raised her arm.

If we can use this way of talking, her hidden feelings, just under the surface, saw in her shoulder a way of expressing themselves without being admitted to consciousness. She could get back at her husband safely and without admitting in any way that that was what she wanted to do. She could express her feelings without knowing what the feelings were in any conscious way.

If the pain got worse, she could ask her husband to hang out the washing, to get things off the top shelves, to do the ironing. She could do that really nicely and apologetically, but he would be being punished. But Emily could not be blamed, or seen as negative in any way. She could be sweet and apologetic and helpful, and bring him a cup of tea at the right moment.

Now the twinge was really there. But if the circumstances had been different, it might have gone as quickly as it came. The question is: what is going on inside, under the surface? There are many psychological theories of how this works, but they all seem to agree in saying that most of our aches and pains have some internal aspect, as well as the more obvious external aspect.

The internal aspect of the pain very often has to do with a conflict inside the person. In Emily's case it was a conflict between her feelings of anger against her husband, and her picture of herself as a nice person who never felt anger.

To say that it is a conflict is to say that two or more parties are fighting – that there is an internal struggle of some kind. So to deal with problems like this we need to have some way of bringing such conflicts out into the open.

In my work as a psychotherapist I see a lot of people like this. And the way I like to work is to say that if the conflict is between two people, let's find out who these people are. So I get out two chairs – or two cushions sometimes, if that's easier – and get the person to sit on one of them. Then I say, 'See if you can imagine that your pain is sitting in the other chair. Then start talking to it.'

At first the person may feel embarrassed about this, or say that it's silly, but I keep on encouraging them, saying things like, 'It could be a character in a play, coming on with a placard that says "Annie's pain", or "Jim's elbow", and speaking on their behalf.' This usually works well enough, and once the person starts, it gets easier as they go along.

Let's follow Emily's dialogue, and see how it worked out.

EMILY: [To pain, in other chair.] I don't like you. Go
                away. What are you doing to me? Go away!

ME: Just remind her of what she's doing to you.

EMILY: You're making my life a misery. I can hardly get
                dressed in the morning. You stop me doing the
                ironing. You stop me hanging out the washing.
                You stop me doing anything high up.

ME: Tell her how you feel towards her.

EMILY: I don't like you. I don't want you. Go away!

ME: Now sit in the other chair and be Emily's pain,
                and talk back. Just take a moment to breathe
                and settle into the part, and then just reply with
                anything that comes.

EMILY'S PAIN: I'm fiery and hot. I'm strong and I don't give up.
                I have long nails and long teeth – I scratch and
                bite. [Emily bared her teeth in a snarl, quite
                unlike her.]

ME: Tell Emily how you feel towards her.

EMILY'S PAIN: You're weak and wishy-washy. You're pale and
                useless. You wouldn't say boo to a goose.

ME: What's your general approach to life?

EMILY'S PAIN: Destruction. I like to destroy things. But I'm
                sharp and clever – I don't get caught. I hide and
                work from behind the scenes. People come close
                and then I *get* them! [Flashing eyes.]

ME: What's your main motive for being here?

EMILY'S PAIN: To protect her. [To Emily.] I'm here to protect
                you. You ought to be grateful to me. I look after
                you. Without me, they'd walk all over you.

ME: Who in particular would walk all over her?

EMILY'S PAIN: Desmond. [The name of Emily's husband.] He
                walks all over you. You're just a doormat for
                him. You let him do it.

ME: Now go back and sit in the other chair, and be
                Emily again. What do you say as Emily?

EMILY: [Long silence.] I don't know what to say. I had
                no idea you were there. I had no idea you felt
                like that.

The session went on for a long time, and it took more than one session to get out all the ramifications and work through all the practical conclusions, but enough has been said to show how this approach can work.

Our pain is always real, but we may be hanging on to it because of our hidden conflicts. By asking the pain to speak and tell us its name, the conflict can be brought out into the open, and dealt with successfully.

What happens in psychodrama, of course, is that the protagonist (client, patient) takes all the roles sooner or later, and experiences each of these parts, from the inside, as that person. This is crucial to all that we have seen so far and all the other approaches to come. We have to get to know the subpersonalities from the inside, by playing them, and not from the outside by observing or describing them.

Although psychodrama is usually conducted in a group, the idea of talking to a subpersonality, and then taking up the role of the subpersonality and talking back, can still be used in an individual way if we want to do so.

THE ORPHEUS EXERCISE

Using ten separate slips of paper, list on each sheet one aspect, trait or attribute of yourself. These may be roles like mother, father, son, worker, policeman, etc. They may be qualities like the happy one, the serene person, the worrier, etc. They may be states of being, behaviour patterns, names or nicknames from the past or present. They may be beliefs, attitudes or any other characteristics. All these ten words or responses are answers to the question 'Who am I?' Do this as rapidly as possible.

Now arrange the ten slips of paper in order of importance to you in the present, with number 1 being the most important and number 10 being the least important. In other words, 1 would be that aspect which defines you best.

Look over these identities and see if you can find any patterns. Do they group together? For example, do any three of them seem to describe or round out a definite character? See, also, if there are any surprises in the list.

Now begin to imagine that you remove each one of these aspects of self, starting with 10 and going all the way through them, including 1 at the end. It may be like peeling an onion. That is, after 10 is removed, then 9, and so forth – each aspect being a layer of the onion. Stop at each one and really experience what it is like not to have it. Imagine what life would be like if you didn't have each of these identities in turn.

When you have fully experienced what it is like not to have any of these identities, you can have one of them back. Notice which one you want back first, and carry on in the same way, each time noticing which one comes next. Did they come back in the reverse order they went, or in some other order? What does this tell you about your priorities?

Allow some time to digest what you have learned. Perhaps write down any insights you get from it.

This can be a deep exercise, or a superficial one – it all depends on you.

Chapter 16

How do we get our subpersonalities to encounter one another?

Gestalt therapy

Psychodrama allows many aspects of a person to be represented and to have dialogues. But someone who laid all the stress on the internal conflicts rather than on the external conflicts was the inventor of Gestalt therapy, Fritz Perls. Perls made a general practice of having an empty chair beside him, in individual or group therapy, on which to place the various members of our internal world. This makes it easy for us to talk to them, and let them talk to us, or to each other. Something that often comes out is a topdog and an underdog.

The topdog is righteous and authoritarian; he knows best. He is sometimes right, but always righteous. He manipulates with demands and threats of catastrophe. The underdog manipulates by being defensive, apologetic, wheedling, playing the crybaby, and so on. The underdog is the Mickey Mouse. The topdog is the Super Mouse. This is the basis for a self-torture game which is common to many people.

The topdog is of course very reminiscent of the Freudian superego, and works in very much the same way as we saw in Chapter 13. But Perls pointed out that Freud never said anything very much about the equally prevalent and problematic underdog. The self-torture game referred to here is simply the way in which we very often entertain 'shoulds' which we do not really intend to honour. We carry them round with us, and every now and then they beat us over the head with the thought, 'I still haven't written to my grandmother', or whatever it may be. The reply is something like, 'I will do it, but I haven't got time at the moment.' In Perls's terms this is the topdog and underdog at work.

This of course lays the major emphasis on conscious experience in the present. However, Gestalt therapy also allows for earlier and unconscious formations of subpersonalities. This it calls working with unfinished business, the completion of the uncompleted.

As we saw earlier, the unfinished business of our childhood gives us some of our subpersonalities, and these are the ones which Gestalt therapy usually leads us to. But it is not restricted to these.

So far we have talked mainly in terms of persons, whether male, female or mythological. Gestalt therapy is more flexible, however, in enabling us to give a voice to the most unlikely candidates. First of all, as in the psychodrama example described in Chapter 15, we can talk to, and talk back as, parts of our own bodies. If there is a pain in some part of our body, we may talk to the pain, and talk back as the pain. Usually when this is done, it turns out that the pain, or the part of the body, was actually standing for one of the more important subpersonalities, and was, as it were, its disguise for the day. This does of course throw a whole different light on the body. It seems to us at first that the person must be single because the body is single. But if the body is itself multiple, that puts another complexion on things.

Fritz Perls was extremely flexible in the entities he was prepared to put on to the empty chair, including such things as: 'your inhibitions'; phoniness; 'your smirk'; 'the old man you saw when you were five and a half'; 'that memory'; 'the dream you didn't have'; the mountain trail; the car number plate; the pillar in the station; the railway station; the water in the vessel; the statue in the lake; the rug on the floor; the two rooms talking to each other; 'your left hand'; Fritz – all these things could be talked to and could talk back. And as they did so, they turned into subpersonalities – sometimes quite familiar subpersonalities and sometimes new and surprising subpersonalities. And as the dialogue progresses, something changes, something moves.

SYMBOL OF A PROBLEM

Have some colours and a sheet of paper ready. Follow the guided fantasy instructions on p. 76.

Now let your attention go to an area of your body which you are particularly aware of or concerned about at the moment. Choose the first part which comes to mind. Take a minute to imagine you are breathing into that area and bringing it to mind even more. Notice everything about it. Let it really be what it is. Let it come to focus.

Now let a symbol come into your mind which represents that focus. It could be a human, animal or plant symbol or an object or geometric shape, or a scene – go with the first symbol which comes up, however unlikely. Notice the details of the symbol, such as colour, movement, shape, texture and anything else which may strike you. Take the colours and the sheet of paper and draw the symbol, not worrying at all about whether it does justice to the symbol as you imagined it – it is just as a reminder to help with the next stage.

Open your eyes and put two cushions on the floor, about three feet apart. Choose one to be yourself, and one to be the symbol. Put the paper under the cushion you have chosen. Now sit on the cushion and be the symbol. By some miracle the symbol can talk, so start by describing yourself. Let your body move as you talk, in an expressive way to get into being the symbol more. Notice how you feel as the symbol.

Move to the other cushion. Now speak as yourself addressing that symbol. Say how you feel about it, perhaps what worries you about it, or what you want from it. Carry on that dialogue, back and forth between the two cushions, until some clarity emerges. Before you finish, make sure you ask the symbol what it needs, and wait for the answer. See if you can give it what it needs, in some way. You may need to think creatively and freshly at this point, but the symbol will make this easier.

Write down any insights which you get from this exercise.

(1) Do you think you do enough?

Yes	0
Most of the time	1
I often wonder	2
No	3

(2) Do you think you are close to having an ulcer?

No	0
I don't think so, but I'm not sure	1
I think I probably am	2
I already have an ulcer	3

(3) How many hours a day do you work?

6 or under	0
7–9	1
10–12	2
13 or more	3

(4) If someone asks you to do something for them, and it is within your power, do you agree to do it?

Only if I really want to for other reasons as well	0
Yes, if it does not take me too far out of my way	1
Yes, if I reasonably can	2
Yes	3

(5) Make a list of all the things that you should have done in the past week but did not have time for because you were too busy. Add to this list the other things you would be able to do if you had more time. How many items have you got on your list?

None	0
Between 1 and 5	1
Between 6 and 10	2
Over 10	3

How to score

This is to discover if you have a Pusher subpersonality. This is sometimes called the Topdog.

0–5   You do not have a Pusher, and that is quite a relief.
6–10 You do have a Pusher, but it is not too prominent and dominant.

11–15 You have a strong Pusher, and this needs to be watched, because it can lead to ill-health and broken relationships. The children of a Pusher always suffer from it.

Chapter 17

How do we transform our subpersonalities?
Psychosynthesis

One of the first people to have started really making use of
subpersonalities for therapy and personal growth was Roberto
Assagioli. He introduced his system of psychosynthesis, which in
some ways follows Jung and in some ways goes further, in the
years after 1910, and opened up his Institute in 1926. Nowadays
psychosynthesis forms one of the main schools working with
subpersonalities, actually under that title.

Psychosynthesis says there are in each of us a diversity of these
subpersonalities, striving to express themselves. So one of the
easiest and most basic ways to facilitate our growth is to get to
know our subpersonalities. The Hag, the Mystic, the Materialist,
the Idealist, the Claw, the Pillar of Strength, the Sneak, the
Religious Fanatic, the Sensitive Listener, the Crusader, the
Doubter, the Grabbie, the Frightened Child, the Poisoner, the
Struggler, the Tester, the Shining Light, the Bitch Goddess, the
Great High Gluck, the Dummy – these are just a few of the names
which people have spontaneously come up with.

Psychosynthesis says that subpersonalities exist at various
levels of organization, complexity and refinement. No specific
cluster or combination of subpersonalities can be considered to be
central for everyone. In working with subpersonalities it is often
found useful to think in terms of a five-phase process.

The first phase is simple recognition – the subpersonality has
to emerge in some way. As we have seen, this may be through the
emergence of a conflict within the person. It may be through a
dream or vision or guided fantasy. Or it may be through splitting
an existing subpersonality into two. But however it comes, the
first thing to do is to realize that it is there.

Phase two is acceptance. All this means is that you have to be willing to work with the subpersonality. It does not mean that at this stage you have to like the subpersonality. Or it may mean the acceptance of one subpersonality by another subpersonality.

This makes possible the third phase, of co-ordination. This means the discovery of the relationships between the subpersonalities. Once they are discovered, they can be worked through. Perhaps there may be interpersonal difficulties between two or more of the subpersonalities. In such a case, some process of conflict resolution may need to be worked out. Since conflict resolution is not always possible, we may have to go for second-best answers such as accommodation or time-sharing. This process may bring about some valuable change on the part of one or more of the subpersonalities.

This then leads on to the fourth phase, of integration. Here we go further with the process of resolving conflicts among the subpersonalities and enabling them to work together in a way which now is harmonious rather than fragmented or disjunctive or negative. During this phase, if the previous phases have been difficult, it may be necessary to make a very bold move. Suppose that we have discovered a part of ourselves which seems thoroughly bad. We are afraid of it and hate it. Nothing seems to get near it. It does not want to accommodate or share time or any of those things. We may in the end have to take a big risk. It may ultimately mean a moment of daring where we take what may seem the enormous risk of entering into and being the very thing we have most hated and feared for many years. And at this point it will transform into its positive form. It will suddenly change into something colourful and completely acceptable. This is one of the magical moments in working with subpersonalities.

The fifth phase is one of synthesis. This is the last phase of the harmonization process, and it leads to the discovery of the Transpersonal Self, and the realization that that is the final truth of the person, not the subpersonalities. This places unity at the end of the road. We shall see later on, as we have briefly already in our mention of people like James Hillman and Mary Watkins, that we do not always have to strive for unity, but it is a strong value within psychosynthesis.

One woman discovered within herself three characters – the Hag, the Doubter and the Idealist. The Hag was critical and twisted, always finding faults and difficulties. The Doubter was afraid and mistrusting, and could never bear to take any risks or

THE OLD HAG

THE DOUBTER

The Idealist

be assertive. And the Idealist had unrealistic ideals, refused to accept her limitations, and had a spirituality which was pretentious and desperate.

In the course of the session, another character appeared, who was not so clear at first, a greater self, a higher self. This higher self looked at the others and saw them very clearly for what they were. The therapist then suggested that the Hag, the Doubter and the Idealist go for a climb up a mountain, watched by the higher self. When they reach the top of the mountain, the higher self sees them looking at one another and leaning in together and flowing into one. A new person is formed. The woman says: 'And she has a bearing that's not puffed up, or on an ego trip, but sure of herself, knowing who she is. She's very, very solid.' The woman then goes into this new character and becomes her. There is some further work in this session, and a good deal of consolidation and working through after the session, but that is the main gist of what happens.

Obviously things do not always go as smoothly or easily as this, but it is a good example to show the basic movement which psychosynthesis aims at.

One of the things we have to notice about psychosynthesis is the way in which it has a place for the Transpersonal Self. And it even has an excercise for approaching this which may be of interest. It is called the disidentification exercise. We repeat to ourselves these words:

I have a body, but I am not my body.
I have feelings, but I am not my feelings.
I have desires, but I am not my desires.
I have thoughts, but I am not my thoughts.
I am I, a centre of pure consciousness and will.

This is the opposite of working with subpersonalities, but it is an important part of the process in psychosynthesis.

CAVE CREATURE

This is a guided fantasy, so refer back to the general instructions for this on p. 76.

Imagine that it is twilight and you are in a wooded area in front of the mouth of a cave. Really get a sense of being there.

There is a sound from inside the cave. You have the feeling that someone or something is going to come out of it. You hide yourself behind the thick trunk of a nearby tree, and wait.

The twilight is thickening. You hear another sound. A figure comes out of the cave. Who or what is it? Give enough time for the figure to show itself fully. How do you feel?

Do you come out from hiding? Is there any meeting or exchange between you and the figure? What happens?

When you feel finished with that, open your eyes and write down what happened, in fine detail. Look back and see what you can learn from it all. Sometimes the figure expresses some suppressed or undeveloped areas of the personality. Could this be so here? If so, what would happen if you allowed it to come out more in everyday life? Could you have a dialogue with it as in one of the earlier exercises?

Chapter 18

How many subpersonalities have we got?

Transactional analysis and ego-state therapy

Transactional analysis, usually known as TA, is well known through such popular books as *I'm OK, You're OK* and *Games People Play*. Its inventor was Eric Berne, who got some of his ideas from the work of Paul Federn, an old psychoanalyst. He and others call subpersonalities ego states.

He argues that as we develop greater complexity of living, our own personality divides into many functions. These are related to one another but also isolated from one another. We divide our self into patterns of behaviour and experience appropriate for various situations. At the same time we push away reactions that would not be adaptive. Who wants to worry about a mathematics test at a party, or plan one's budget at a football game?

Berne calls these patterns ego states, and they are normally a part of us all. One of the most famous examples of this is, of course, the idea that we all have within us a parent, an adult and a child, and that these can sometimes be in conflict with one another. These answer in every way to our description of subpersonalities. Faced with a cream bun, our Parent subpersonality may say 'Put it back!', our Adult may say 'Better not', and our Child may say 'Go on, have it right now!' The conflicts may, of course, be much more serious than that, as we shall see later on.

Berne says that these ego states or subpersonalities may get organized into scripts. These scripts are laid down, often in our childhood. They may be like fairy stories; sometimes they are like horror stories. We live with these scripts and hold on to them firmly. They represent our story, our myth as to why we are the way we are. Some scripts are quite crippling, and we may have to learn how to give them up. One of the key steps on the way is to get to know each character in the story, and what part they play.

This we can do by taking each character as a subpersonality.

NURTURING PARENT

Imagine that sitting opposite you is your Nurturing Parent. This is a character who loves you unconditionally. This character has immense compassion and never gets irritable or moody or impatient. This selfless love has always been there for you, though you may not have been aware of it. Often you have sought substitutes for it elsewhere, and been frustrated when it did not work out. You have made mistakes, but your Nurturing Parent is not hurt by that: the Nurturing Parent cares, but does not mind. Now you can make any statement, ask any question, make any demand you like. What do you say to this person? And what do they say back? Carry on this dialogue as long as you need to. Write down any thoughts which come to you afterwards.

SHAPIRO

At about the same time, Stewart Shapiro was starting to work out his practice of using what he called subselves in therapy. He says that in his therapy-room there are ten chairs, but they're not set up for group therapy; they're for individual work – one chair for each subpersonality. Sometimes he would use one or two chairs; occasionally three or four; once in a while, all ten.

He introduces a new idea which we have not met with before, though we shall meet it again in the work of Hal Stone and Sidra Winkelman. He believes in deliberately creating a Chairman of the Board. This is a character who will stand outside the rest of the subpersonalities, and make decisions about how to handle them. But he makes it clear that it is no part of the job of this functionary to exclude or eliminate any of the characters.

Unlike Berne, he does have a place for something outside the subpersonalities, and here he comes very close to psychosynthesis. For example, you may uncover various subpersonalities such as those of the person who found a Clown, a Gorilla or Caveman, a Child, an Earth Mother and Father Time. The disidentification exercise (see the end of the previous chapter) in this case would be, 'I have a Clown but I am not a Clown, I have

a Gorilla, but I am not a Gorilla', and so on. After going through all the subselves, the person would say (or think), 'I am I, a centre of pure consciousness and will.' He sees the work with subpersonalities as one way of attaining sufficient psychological harmony so that spiritual harmony can follow. This is very much like psychosynthesis.

THE EGO-STATE SCHOOL

Rather similar to the work of Berne and Shapiro, but taking off in an interesting direction, is the work of the ego-state school, led by John Watkins. These people are prepared to use hypnosis at times in their work, and see this as legitimate. This approach does not seem to have the same emphasis on polarities as does the Gestalt school. They say that fusion, or the merging of two or more personalities into a 'oneness', is generally neither essential nor desirable except in special circumstances.

But they certainly make some new points of their own. They say that subpersonalities, being only parts of a person, frequently think concretely and illogically like a child. It is common for a subpersonality to plot the destruction or death of the person while believing that it itself will survive. So in such a case, suicide is felt to apply to only one of the personalities, not one's self.

This is certainly a useful hint – something to watch out for very carefully. And it may be that working with subpersonalities could make it easier to become aware of this kind of possibility.

HOW MANY SUBPERSONALITIES?

If we now ask how many subpersonalities each person has, TA answers six (with some variations); Shapiro says between four and nine; and the ego-state school has no definite answer on this. TA mainly relies on the two parental ego states – Critical Parent and Nurturing Parent – the single adult ego state, and three child ego states – Adapted Child, Little Professor and Natural Child. Shapiro's list is much the same, except that as we have seen he has a place for a higher self.

Psychosynthesis has no limit on the numbers, and sometimes talks of 'a cast of thousands'. Gestalt therapy again sets no limits, but usually seems to think of subpersonalities as occurring in polarized pairs. Jung again sets no limits, but in practice only refers to a small number of complexes and a slightly larger number of archetypes.

My own view is that four to nine is what we usually find, but that there is nothing fixed about this.

(1) Is it really possible to know what someone else is feeling?
No, it is a philosophical impossibility   0
Occasionally I can be in tune with someone else   1
I think it often is possible   2
It is quite easy, really   3

(2) Is it possible to give somebody something without wanting anything back in return?
No, I don't believe so, if we are honest   0
On occasion, yes   1
I think it often is possible   2
Yes, of course   3

(3) Is it possible to do things for people without wanting to control them?
No, not if we really examine ourselves   0
Sometimes, yes   1
Quite often, yes   2
Yes, definitely – I do it all the time   3

(4) Is it possible to love someone unconditionally?
No, it is pie in the sky   0
Rare but possible   1
I do hope so   2
Yes, definitely – I find it possible   3

(5) Can a person be loving and genuine at the same time?
No, they are two quite different and separate things   0
Occasionally, yes   1
I think so   2
Yes, they are really the same thing deep down   3

(6) Can a person be strong and vulnerable at the same time?
No, they are quite opposite things   0
I am not sure, perhaps, sometimes   1
I have had some experiences which seemed like this   2
Yes, definitely, I have integrated them together   3

How to score

This is to discover whether you have a Nurturing Parent subpersonality.

0–6   You do not have a Nurturing Parent, or if you do it is well hidden or under severe control. Why not cultivate it a bit more?

7–12   You do have a Nurturing Parent, but it does not come out all the time, and you may have difficulty finding it at times.

13–18 You do have a Nurturing Parent, and are in good contact with it. The only thing you have to watch out for is being exploited or used by people who find this out. But you should be able to handle this, because of your accurate perception of others.

Chapter 19

Does everyone have the same subpersonalities?
Voice dialogue

And this leads us on to what is perhaps the most ambitious and well-worked-out approach to subpersonalities yet devised. Like Berne and Shapiro, the voice dialogue people like to give names and categories to the subpersonalities. They are Hal Stone and Sidra Winkelman, who come from a Jungian background, but have now broken away to found their own school. They have a lot more to say than any of the others as to all the ins and outs of actually working with subpersonalities. We have already met some of the characters they discovered. Of course, not everyone has all of these:

the Protector/Controller
the Pusher
the Critic
the Perfectionist
the Power Brokers (Power, Ambition, Pusher, Money,
Selfishness, etc., all seen as subpersonalities)
the Pleaser
the Inner Child
the Good and Bad Mother
the Good and Bad Father

Stone and Winkelman use empty chairs or cushions in their work, and encourage the person to come to terms with the sub-personality in question. They encourage an Aware Ego to take responsibility for the dance of the subpersonalities.

One of the perennial questions which therapists get asked is: 'If you are encouraging people to be more powerful in their lives, and to take charge, as you put it, of their lives, is this not going to make them more oppressive and more arrogant?' After quoting a number of concrete cases, our authors make an important distinction between being powerful and being empowered. Being and acting powerful means that we are identified with the energy patterns on the Power side. Empowerment means that we have an Aware Ego that can honour, and to some extent embrace, both Power and, ironically enough, Vulnerability. They say that empowerment is certainly one of the outcomes of their approach.

So a combination of strength and vulnerability – to some people exact opposites – seems to be a good way of looking at empowerment. And once we have seen it in this way, we can appreciate how particularly relevant this concept is to women. In a way, women are more likely to seek empowerment than men. Because they do not have equal access to traditional power, they are forced to work from an empowered position. This means that they have access to power integrated with vulnerability. This is different from a more orthodox power position, involving identification with patriarchal power energies. This again is a question hardly touched on by other writers in this field. Nearly all of them seem to assume that women are going to have just the same types of subpersonalities as men. But this is not necessarily the case at all, and it is good to be reminded of this.

There is in fact in the work of Stone and Winkelman a good appreciation of the special problems of being a woman in the patriarchal society of today. They talk a good deal about the types of subpersonality which it would be most useful for women to cultivate and make familiar. One of these is the Warrior. Not the kind of warrior which may spring to mind with a spear and shield, stamping and grimacing, but the kind of warrior we have become acquainted with through the work of Carlos Castaneda, Hyemenyosts Storm and others. Until recently, warrior energy was considered unfeminine or castrating to men. We can now clearly see how necessary it is for self-protection, and how powerless a woman can be if this energy is disowned.

Men and women alike need warrior energy to protect themselves. Needless to say, women are seen as life-givers and healers, and the thought that they might have any destructive energies is potentially intimidating. But to deny our destructive energies, whether male or female, is to deny a major power source. Sadly, such denial often causes destructive energy to be projected on to men.

Interestingly, this voice has been so thoroughly repressed in women that it rarely assumes the form of a woman or girl as a subpersonality. It is far more likely to come out in dreams and visions as a jungle cat, a graceful feline killer.

So we have here a good awareness of the way in which we are living in a particular historical epoch, in a particular part of the world, with a particular subculture. They are telling us that we have to take into account the social context within which all therapy is done.

PICTURE DIALOGUE

Many people nowadays have a pack of Tarot cards. If you don't, you could do this exercise using pictures out of magazines, or picture postcards. Pick out one card (or picture) you like very much, and one which you dislike very much. Imagine that it has a character, and can talk as that character. Put each one on or under a cushion or chair. Then sit on each one in turn, and have a dialogue between them. Which one would speak first? What would they say to the other one? What would the answer be? Continue with this dialogue until some useful terminus is reached.

(1) If someone bumps into you, or treads on your toe, or pushes in front of you, do you object?

Yes	0
Sometimes	1
Usually not	2
No	3

(2) If someone asks you to do something for them, and it is within your power, do you agree to do it?

Only if I really want to for other reasons as well	0
Yes, if it does not take me too far out of my way	1
Yes, if I reasonably can	2
Yes	3

(3) If two people you know well are having a heated argument, does it upset you?

No	0
A little bit, yes	1
Yes, it does, rather	2
Yes, very much, and I have to try to stop it	3

(4) Is it wrong to show anger and aggression?

No	0
I think so sometimes	1
In most cases, yes	2
Always	3

(5) How important is it to you that the people you meet and interact with should like you?

Not important at all	0
Some importance to me	1
It is important	2
It is a must, and I feel bad if they don't	3

How to score

This is to discover whether you have a Pleaser subpersonality. This is sometimes called the Adapted Child ego state.

0–5   You do not have a Pleaser subpersonality, and so do not need to worry about this possibility.

6–10   You do have a Pleaser, but it may not cause you too many problems. Do keep an eye on it, in case it takes over more.

11–15 You have a strong Pleaser, and this is liable to cause you some suffering along the way. See if you can question it, and bring it down to a more reasonable size. This is well worth working on.

Chapter 20

Can hypnotism help?

Hypnotherapy and neuro-linguistic programming

There has been a great deal of interest in subpersonalities in recent years in the field of hypnotherapy. Various types and grades of hypnotic trance are used in conjunction with other forms of psychotherapy.

An interesting point mentioned by John Beahrs, an excellent writer in this field, is that the therapist may not actually need to deal with each subpersonality in detail. He gives the example of a patient he had who was dealt with on the basis of just one subpersonality, which was worked with very thoroughly and a good outcome resulted. Later, this patient was able to report an awareness of five distinct subpersonalities, all dating back to childhood. These had come together successfully without having been dealt with separately by the therapist.

Another point comes from the work of Ralph Allison, who classifies subpersonalities into three categories – persecutors, rescuers and internal self-helpers. The first two of these are relatively familiar, but the internal self-helpers were new to me. According to Allison, they have characteristics differing from pathological subpersonalities and are a great potential resource in treatment. In his view, they differ in having (1) no identifiable time and reason for their formation; (2) no defensive function; and (3) far more accuracy of perception than the normal conscious person. They are incapable of distorted perception, and therefore able to tell a therapist all his mistakes. This is fascinating if true, and certainly something worth looking out for and exploring in more detail.

In general, work with subpersonalities is no more common in hypnotherapy than it is in other forms of therapy. John and Helen Watkins are two people who have taken this approach a very long way. They make the point that working with ego states is like a kind of family therapy. This is, I feel, a very fruitful thought.

They also give the example of a student who could not study successfully. At a conscious ego level, he wanted to study and was very upset when he could not do so. However, another ego state, identified as a four-year-old child, wanted more play and less study. He refused to let the student study unless he was treated better. The therapist made friends with the child, and persuaded him to play at night, thus permitting the student to study during the day. A week later the client came back saying that he had studied well and passed an important examination: but he wondered why he was having such vivid dreams, in full colour, every night. It turned out that the child had kept his agreement and was playing at night. The student was not aware of this ego state until the therapist informed him about it.

So this is very interesting work, and I have acquired a new respect for at least some aspects of hypnotherapy since coming across it.

NLP

An approach which we need to say somewhat less about is that of neuro-linguistic programming (NLP). Genie Laborde talks about subpersonalities, and makes rather a nice point about them – that inner conflicts are evidence of our potential flexibility. She points out that the incongruence we so often notice in people (the tone of voice not matching what is being said, or the gestures not fitting with what is being expressed verbally, etc.) can very often be traced back to conflicting subpersonalities. These are within the person, some of them quite possibly unconscious.

And she states very succinctly and well the main point of becoming aware of one's subpersonalities. By becoming aware of our internal conflicts (such as over anger, for example), we can release the mental energy we have been using for repression. This means that we can work out some internal negotiations, and use the released energy in our lives.

What we then get, she says, is congruence – the co-operation of our various parts working in harmony, so that it is the whole person acting at once.

TALK TO YOUR ANGER

Put your anger on another chair or cushion, and talk to it. You can ask it any question, put points to it, make demands on it, anything. Very often it is good to start by reminding it of a couple of times when it came up and caused problems. Once you have got well started and said a few things to it, swap over and be the anger, and talk back. What do you want to say, as the anger? It may be something by way of an answer to the questions which have been asked, or it may be something quite different. Let yourself really take up the position of being the anger, and do not control what is said – let it be as genuine and spontaneous as possible.

Try the same thing with your guilt, fear, worry, courage or hope, or any other characteristic of this kind which seems to be relevant to you.

Chapter 21

Subpersonalities in the astrological chart

Greene and Sasportas

This kind of outcome is also found in another rather similar way of working, developed by Liz Greene and Howard Sasportas. They feel that the astrological chart has a careful and specific delineation of influences. Some of these are upon the person and some have to do with conflicts within the person. Either way, they can be used to identify subpersonalities and suggest how they may be worked with.

They point out that there is an important difference between being a subpersonality and having a subpersonality. They say that if you are a dog that bites, then you bite. But if you have a dog that bites, then you can choose to let it bite, or choose to put a muzzle on the dog, or teach it not to bite. If you are totally identified with a subpersonality, then you just act it out. But if you realize a subpersonality is something you have operating in you, then you can do something to change, alter or transform it.

Their outlook is rather Jungian, and they make an interesting and novel suggestion. Jung says that each person (or Persona) has a Shadow, a negative or inferior subpersonality. This character embodies all the worst things we do not like or accept about ourselves. Greene and Sasportas suggest that perhaps each of the subpersonalities has its own shadow. So for example, someone with a strong love subpersonality might be harbouring resentment and anger: 'When is it my turn for someone to give to me and look after me for a change?' Or a strong masculine or Animus subpersonality may have a fear of not being loved or appreciated hidden within it.

This is an interesting thought, and it does often happen that when one is working with one subpersonality, another voice will come through, and another subpersonality will advance and

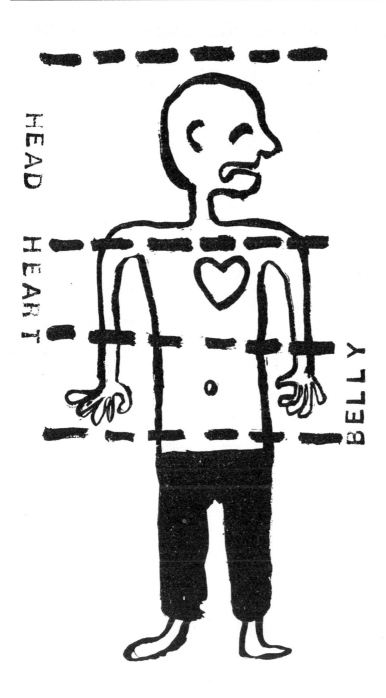

have to be recognized. Sometimes this may be a shadow aspect of the same subpersonality, and sometimes it may be describable in some other way. But certainly the idea of a shadow for each subpersonality is a thought worth playing with.

They also have a discussion of the question of whether there are any standard subpersonalities, so to speak, which come up in all people at all times. They have found some of these, and consider the main ones to be the Critic (Judge), the Saboteur (Victim, Martyr) and the Inner Child. These, they say, come up so often that they may be universal. As we have seen in other chapters, there are many who would agree with this.

But for the most part they do not like this solution, but would prefer to speak of certain conflicts which may appear quite regularly. The first of these is the conflict between subpersonalities which have love at their core, and other subpersonalities which have will at their core. Other typical conflicts they deal with are between those subpersonalities with change at their core versus those with maintenance at their core; those who are devoted to work versus those who are more interested in play. Again there is often a split between those who have high ideals and want to pursue them at all costs and the pragmatists who just want to make sure that things work, at a reasonable cost. And again there can be a split between those who love freedom and those who are convinced that closeness is more important. Finally there can be the disagreements between head, heart and belly, where there is often a permanent tension.

As with others working in this field, what they do is to personify each side of the argument, giving each character a position, and letting it speak for itself.

ACTIVE AND PASSIVE

Write two brief sketches, in one of which you are active, initiating the events which happen and controlling them, while in the other you are passive, having something done to you and being controlled. When you have written the two tales, put one of them in a chair, and the other in a chair opposite to it, so that the two chairs are facing each other, about three feet apart.

Now sit on one chair and be the person in that story, and talk to the other one. When it seems right, switch over and sit in the other chair, and answer back as the other person. Let this dialogue continue until you learn something from it.

If you are into astrology, you can use this exercise to contrast two signs (or planets, or houses) in your chart which affect you differently.

Chapter 22

The history of subpersonalities
From early cultures to today

Most primitive cultures, both ancient and modern, have been aware of what we have been calling the continuum of dissociation, from altered states of consciousness to moods to subpersonalities to spirit possession to multiple personality. Priests, witch-doctors and shamans have made these ideas a stock in trade since early in the history of the human race. There were 'sleep temples' in Ancient Greece and in Egypt where patients were encouraged to go into altered states of consciousness, were actually hypnotized or were talked to during their sleep and given curative suggestions. In primitive cultures, these changes have often been brought about through the use of trances, and trance induction has been brought about by means of repetitious rhythm, drums, dancing, chanting, etc.

ANCIENT EGYPT

The earliest example I have come across of someone actually talking to a subpersonality, and being answered back, comes in an Egyptian document of approximately 2200 BC – a dialogue between a suicidal man and his soul. This is a moving document, which still makes sense to us today.

ANCIENT GREECE

In his book the *Republic*, written in Ancient Greece, Plato speaks of three parts to the psyche: the rational, the appetitive (concerned with bodily needs such as hunger and thirst) and the spirited one. Again we can recognize what he is talking about here – these ideas do not sound strange to us. In another book, the

Phaedrus, he speaks more concretely of a three-part psyche, imaged as a charioteer and two horses. The charioteer guides the chariot and makes decisions about the destination. One horse is a lover of honour, modesty and temperance, who seems to be prudent and restrained; the other a crooked, lumbering animal with insolence, pride and impulsiveness, who seems to be the voice of instinct. This again sounds familiar.

THE MIDDLE AGES

Many later thinkers had different versions of this type of approach, and in the Middle Ages the problem of the unity of personality had already been pondered over by St Augustine in his *Confessions*. Considering the change that had taken place in him since his conversion, Augustine remarked that his old pagan personality, of which nothing seemed to remain in his waking state, still must exist since it was revived at night and in his dreams. This brings Augustine to discuss the problem of the dreamer's moral responsibility for his dreams. Augustine also emphasized the fact that memories from early infancy, which we had thought to be entirely lost, can reappear, as if our brains retain traces of all that we have previously experienced.

In the twelfth century, a man called Hugh de St Victor wrote a dialogue with the soul. This reads very much like our own dialogues with our subpersonalities in therapy.

More dramatic, of course, is the idea of spirit possession. For centuries this was the only way of explaining how someone could be 'taken over' by another spirit, another personality. In possession the appearance of the person could change, the voice could change, and the whole emotional range of the person could extend. Possession in the most negative sense only exists in countries and at times which believe in the Devil, or at least in demons.

The phenomenon of possession, so frequent for many centuries, is not really what we mean by a subpersonality: as we saw in an earlier chapter, possession is further along on the continuum of dissociation. But in an age of superstition, where it was difficult to make such fine distinctions, many things could have been labelled as possession which are more like the ordinary use of subpersonalities in our terms.

THE EIGHTEENTH CENTURY

Similarly, in this book we are not much concerned with hypnosis, but it is a fact that the unconscious was explored by hypnotists (mesmerists, magnetizers, etc.) for 150 years or so before psychotherapy as we know it came on the scene.

As has been pointed out, the concept of the unconscious had to come first, and the concept of dual personality actually came before the idea of subpersonalities considered as something within the normal range of variation for human beings. We can even pinpoint a year (1784) when the idea of the unconscious came into the sphere of psychology, through the work of the Comte de Puységur.

THE NINETEENTH CENTURY

At the start of the nineteenth century, the philosopher Herbart (with whose work Freud was well acquainted) was already talking about the psychology of internal conflict, the unconscious and repression.

During the nineteenth century the first dynamic psychiatry began to develop. In this body of work a new model of the human mind was evolved. It was based on the duality of the conscious and unconscious minds. Later, it was modified to the form of a cluster of subpersonalities underlying the conscious personality. In the latter part of the nineteenth century the concepts of the autonomous activity of split fragments of personality arose.

And at the same time there came about a recognition of the mythopoetic function of the mind – the way in which the mind could continually create stories, myths, legends and fantasies. The mythopoetic function (a term apparently coined by Myers in about 1900) works through the imagination, and involves the loosening of ego boundaries and the use of many different frames of reference. In this conception the unconscious seems to be continually concerned with creating fictions which sometimes remain unconscious or appear only in dreams. Sometimes they take the form of daydreams, and sometimes a subpersonality is created.

The first psychologist I can find who dealt with the idea in a way which seems to throw off the historical distortions was William James, but he really said very little about where they came from or how they worked. He started working on his great book on the principles of psychology in about 1878, and it was published in 1890. In it he talked about social selves, and reckoned that people had many social selves, each of which could be called up in an appropriate situation.

THE 1890s

Starting with the discoveries of Charles Richet, Hippolyte Taine and Gabriel Tarde, in the latter years of the nineteenth century, the unconscious became an active part of the personality as well as a reservoir of the emotions and of forgotten or repressed facts. We have here a very different conception of the unconscious, one which is remarkably close to the Freudian concept.

In 1892 the famous psychologist Alfred Binet published a book on alterations in personality in which he said that in a large number of people several distinct consciousnesses arise, each of which may have perceptions, a memory and even a moral character of its own. This was a remarkable observation for its time. Binet came to the conclusion that what we know about ourselves is but a part, perhaps a very small part, of what we are.

In 1895, Theodule Ribot published a book which explicitly denied the existence of a superordinate self and postulated the existence of multiple selves.

In 1897, J.M. Baldwin published the first social psychology text, and in it gave some credence to the possibility of multiple selves, based on social conditioning.

In the field of philosophy, too, there was an interest at this time, and one of the most eloquent statements was made by the British Hegelian, William Wallace, when he said:

> We have hardly formed our resolve when we regret it: the voices of our other selves, of that manifold pack of half-formed personalities within us, none of which we dare honestly disown, are raised in protest against the usurping monarchy of our overt resolve.

THE TWENTIETH CENTURY

And so we come into the early years of the present century. In 1904, Sidis and Goodhart said the multiple personality was just an exaggerated expression of something which was actually quite normal in the human personality. Different selves are elicited by different situations.

In the early years of this century there was an upsurge of a literature concerned with subtler descriptions of the many facets of human personality, and their interplay. The major figure in this upsurge was Marcel Proust, who maintained that the personality can be 'composed of many little egos, distinct though side by side'. But other authors, such as Pirandello, Joyce and Woolf, shared an interest in the unconscious in its many manifestations. No longer primarily emphasizing the obvious aspects of unconscious phenomena as seen in hypnotism and dual personality, they were interested instead in the many facets of personality in all of us. Personality changes from moment to moment, depending on place, time and our companions. There is no one 'real' ego, but rather a succession of egos, or the alternating dominance of different aspects of the ego. Virginia Woolf has her character Bernard say: 'I am not one person: I am many people.'

These literary pursuits were paralleled by work in psycho-therapy, as we saw in an earlier chapter. Jung was talking about the complexes as early as 1908, and had much more to say about them from his experiments with word association. Freud was very interested in this work, but did not come up with his division into the it, the I and the over-I until the 1920s. I would describe the over-I (superego) as a complex, and as a typical subpersonality.

In 1924, the concept had been taken into psychiatry by Eugen Bleuler, who said in his textbook of psychiatry that the complexes can actually acquire subpersonalities with some sort of independence of the psyche. But psychiatry apparently did not retain this insight, and in today's texts no such admission is found.

In 1936, Kurt Lewin published his book on topological psychology, in which he said that regions of the personality could become relatively independent, and that their connectedness could vary considerably. He was clear that all this could be observed in the normal person, and was not necessarily patho-logical at all. This is a very important insight, but it was never followed up in psychology generally, in spite of the great respect in which Lewin was held.

Since then there has been a burgeoning quantity of different applications of this general idea, many of which we have now looked at. All I wanted to do here was to outline in a brief way the early steps in the process.

Chapter 23

Recent thinking on subpersonalities
Psychologists, brain researchers and philosophers have their say

One of the most exciting developments of recent years in relation to subpersonalities is the way in which they have been adopted by academic psychology. This makes them into something more than a curiosity. But this is not all. The idea has also been admitted into the computer theory of artificial intelligence, and translated into terms of hardware and software. Further still, the idea of subpersonalities has invaded the field of philosophy. Let us look at some of the contributors to this, and find out what they are saying.

ACADEMIC PSYCHOLOGY

Colin Martindale investigated this by looking at the structure of subpersonalities (which he calls subselves) within the personality. One obvious line of inquiry was simply to ask people about their subselves. This is certainly possible, and people generally give positive answers to this kind of question. This meant that the structure could be built up quite readily. A number of interesting implications of this model were drawn out by him. He showed that cognitive theory (so popular today in academia) could be much enriched by such a way of seeing the world.

T.B. Rogers used the concept of a prototype. This is a schema of the self which is available to consciousness. The elements of the prototype are self-descriptive terms such as traits, values and possibly even memories of specific behaviours and events. This means talking about emotions and feelings. If all we can talk about is the intellect, clearly this is not going to be enough to describe a human being (though it may be fine for describing a computer). Emotion directs the person's attention towards a specific event. For instance, an example of kindness may not be noticed by a subpersonality centred on independence, but for one with kindness at the centre it would evoke a feeling, thereby drawing the person's attention to it.

Hazel Markus, together with her colleague Keith Sentis, developed the notion of self-schemas, which we have already come across, as her version of subpersonalities. What is a schema, exactly? She says that schemas are the central cognitive units in the human information-processing system. She sees schemas as memory structures and conceptual frameworks, and makes the very important point that a schema has a dual nature: a schema is at once a *structure* and a *process*. Having established the notion of a schema, Markus and her colleague go on to say that some of these schemas have to do with the self. In other words, they have to do with the system as a whole.

So from their perspective, the self can be conceptualized as a system of self-schemas. A schema integrates all the information known about the self in a given behavioural domain into a systematic framework. A schema can potentially represent the two distinct aspects of the self – the self as the *knower* and the self as that which is *known*. Self-schemas are generalizations about the self. It is very exciting to see the idea of a subpersonality being used in so creative and so productive a way.

Seymour Rosenberg and Michael Gara asked people to describe, in their own terms, each of twenty to fifty personal identities, one at a time, and to list as exhaustively as possible the characteristics and feelings associated with each of these. This was done in quite a complex way, and the interviews took several hours to complete, spread over several sittings. They covered negative as well as positive subpersonalities (which they call identities), which is of course important in this work. They are open-ended rather than giving predetermined responses to choose from.

In one investigation the subjects were asked of each identity, 'If you were to wake up one morning and find that this identity had been taken away or lost its significance, to what extent would your life be affected?' The researchers were then able to test whether this subjective importance rating tied in with the other interviews. In most cases it did. In those cases where it did not, the person was in fact going through some sort of crisis of identity. In this book, we have used just such an exercise in

Chapter 15, from which you can see how dramatic and challenging a task it can be.

The authors of this paper also show how the same approach can be adopted in relation to existing sources of information such as diaries, letters and literary material. They carried out an analysis of Thomas Wolfe's novel *Look Homeward, Angel* to show how this may be achieved. This analysis was then compared with a psycho-biography of Thomas Wolfe, and a convincing correspondence was found.

Dan McAdams looked at the development of ego identity in the life of George Bernard Shaw. He says there are three central protagonists in Shaw's life-story – the Snob, the Noisemaker and the Diabolical One. He says that these were more than just roles. These images of self McAdams calls imagos. He says that an imago is an idealized and personified image of self that functions as a main character in an adult's life-story. We would call it a subpersonality.

The author goes on to suggest that imagos are often arranged in the self as polar opposites. This idea is of course also found in Gestalt therapy, as we have seen. It was the general view of Jung, who also agrees with McAdams that the synthesis of opposing imagos is a hallmark of the mature self. His main emphasis, then, is on imagos as main characters in our personal myth – the story we tell to ourselves and others about the meaning of our lives. We have already come across this idea in Chapter 18, but here it is turning up as a result of objective research.

THE BRAIN

The next piece of work on the scene which we need to examine comes from quite a different context – the field of brain research. Michael Gazzaniga is a well-known researcher, particularly in the area of the split brain. This kind of research can be done when the corpus callosum – the bridge between the two sides of the brain – is cut for some surgical reason. Each side of the brain can then be studied separately.

He spells out in detail, with experiments, that evidence accumulates to suggest that the brain is organized into modules, rather than acting as a whole.

He emphasizes that the mind is not an indivisible whole, operating in a single way to solve all problems. Rather, there are many specific and identifiably different modules of the mind dealing with all the information they are exposed to. The vast and rich information impinging on our brains is broken up into parts, and many systems start at once to work on it. And he makes the crucial point that these modular activities frequently operate apart from our conscious verbal selves.

He then raises the important question of where internal conflicts come from. How can we have internal dissension? He suggests it is because our brains are organized in terms of independent modules, each capable of action. Each module can carry out activities that test and retest the beliefs that are being maintained. We are not limited to our dominant left brain's language and cognitive systems. The conflict is produced by a mental module working relatively independently.

In other words, a subpersonality is involved here. The conflict is between two subpersonalities, and that is why it is so lively and personal. It may be worthwhile to underline the fact that no hierarchical structure is being assumed here, and to realize that no hierarchical structure is necessary. Gazzaniga's contribution is to show that subpersonalities are not just a psychological concept, but have an objective anatomical basis.

So how is it that we feel like a single person all the time? He has an answer to that, too. He says that a brain system built in a modular way would also need a single interpreter. This interpreter would explain the various actions of the modules. And he finds that the brain is organized in precisely such a fashion. So here we have a fascinating confirmation, from a different angle again, of the basic idea of subpersonalities and how they work within the individual.

ORNSTEIN

Soon after this came another independent sally into the field, this time from Robert Ornstein. Ornstein has, of course, written a great deal about the brain and consciousness. In this new book he outlines a theory which combines extremely well with what we have found so far. He says that the mind contains a changeable conglomeration of different kinds of 'small minds'. These may include fixed reactions, talents, flexible thinking, many different versions. These different entities are temporarily employed – wheeled into consciousness – and then usually wheeled out again after use.

By mainly talking about the small minds, Ornstein is able to tackle some interesting puzzles. For example, we have all met the case of the person who behaves in ways which are very uncharacteristic. Such a person may actually go against their own espoused rules or principles. What Ornstein says about this is that the small mind operating at any time may not have the appropriate memory in store. It may not have the required behaviour in its repertoire. We may well be able to decide how to behave in a situation when we are calm. In that state we can see many ways of acting. But things are not always calm, and that means that we cannot always do what is necessary as and when it pleases us. The tension of the situation can drive our knowledge out of our heads, so to speak.

The small minds that we think we may choose from may be unavailable to consciousness when we need them. But Ornstein urges that this is not inevitable. Through the process of coming to self-awareness (perhaps through counselling or psychotherapy) it may be possible to acquire more self-control (in the good sense).

It is a question, he says, of who is running the show. In most people, at most times, the automatic system organizes which small mind gets wheeled in. This will most likely be on the automatic basis of blind habit. But there is a point when a person can become conscious of the multiminds. This self-awareness can enable the person to begin to run them, rather than hopelessly watch anger wheel in once again. This is precisely the kind of self-awareness which this book is aiming at.

Nor is this the only question which this approach can tackle. Ornstein comes to the issue of how we relate to other people once we have the notion of small minds clearly in view. It makes it easier to see how we could relate better to people who seem difficult or frustrating to us. We may dislike one part of them, but how about the other parts? Why don't we look on each person as a group or team? We could then dislike one aspect of them, but like others. In a restaurant, we might say, 'I like the food, but not the decor', and in this way neatly separate different functions. This would enable us more easily to decide whether to go to the restaurant again. It could be the same with people. That is perhaps a little optimistic, but at least it shows how we can free up our approaches to other people.

CANTOR AND KIHLSTROM

Much more technical is the next piece of work to come our way, this time from Nancy Cantor and John Kihlstrom. They take the whole idea one step further by postulating the existence of different levels within the subpersonalities, which they call selves. They find that the self-concept, usually spoken of as something unitary, depends in fact upon this system of selves, and they talk about the family of selves.

If we make such a move, the unity of self may then come from the many overlapping resemblances among the different members of the family. Of course some of these selves are more central, more important to 'who you are' than are others. These central selves are more representative of one's self than are those out on the edge. They exhibit many features shared by other selves in the family of selves. And because of this overlap they are closer to the meaning of who we are. Also, these central selves are representative because they more clearly differentiate self from others. The self-concept, therefore, must represent both the *variety* and the *unity* within each person's family of selves. Recent theorists have likened the self-concept to an implicit theory or a network of linked concepts of self.

How does this relate to the idea of a schema, which we came across before? In a very interesting way: these authors say that it is the more central selves which are closer to the idea of a schema. In fact, by concentrating attention on these central selves, they become more vivid. They acquire a richness and a solidity which may be extremely important in the person's life. This concept of centrality can help in the work of acquiring self-knowledge. This now links with the idea of a narrative and a life-story, along the lines suggested by McAdams. It is the personal myth represented by the life-story which links together the different selves and makes sense of the relationships between them.

Thus their idea of selves is much more dynamic than some of what we have come across so far. They broach much more fully the subject of the future projection of the subselves. In other words, we are now allowed to become interested in the possible selves which may appear in the future, and look at the question of how they might affect present-day actions.

MARKUS AND NURIUS

This leads very naturally to the next contribution which appeared, the work of Hazel Markus and Paula Nurius. In it they go into this whole question of possible selves. We are clearly in a much more sophisticated realm of discourse by this time. They say that possible selves are conceptions of the self in future states. The possible selves that are hoped for might include:

the powerful or leader self,
the elegant and glamorous self,
the revered and esteemed self,
the rich and famous self,
the trim, toned, in-shape self.

They go on to say that there are such things as negative possible selves; dreaded possible selves may comprise an equally vivid and compelling set. It might include:

the alone and unwanted self,
the addicted or dependent self,
the violent or aggressive self, or
the undervalued and unrecognized self.

These possible selves, say the authors, have a great deal to do with motivation. They are, in fact, the concrete manifestation of enduring goals, aspirations and motives. They actually provide an essential link between the self-concept and motivation. They are the cognitive bridges between the present and the future.

In other words, they are the positive and negative subpersonalities, and everything in this book is relevant to them.

MINSKY

The last book which has come to my notice is from a quite different origin from any of those I have mentioned so far. It, therefore, constitutes a further independent corroboration of the importance of the idea of subpersonalities in understanding how the human mind actually works.

This is from Marvin Minsky, who is an expert in the field of artificial intelligence. This is a recent outcrop of science which studies how the structure and function of computers can by analogy throw light on how the mind might be organized. In other words, what he is doing is to build up, step by step by logical considerations, what must be involved to make intelligent action possible.

And the final conclusion he comes to is that there must be agents within the mind. These may have more or less responsibility, more or less specifically assigned, and may group together into broader agencies.

After a long but very readable discussion, he comes to a conclusion which he thinks makes sense. This is to say that there exists, inside the brain, a society of different minds. Like members of a family, the different minds can work together to help each other. But each still has its own mental experiences that the others never know about. Several such agencies could have many agents in common. But this would not mean that they had a sense of each other's interior activities. They would be neighbours, rather like people whose apartments share opposite sides of the same walls. The processes that share the brain need not share one another's mental lives.

So here again we have the same message, this time from a quite different field.

This has been a fascinating journey, moving through this world of experiment and observation, questionnaire and survey. We have put together much research from many different sources. We can see that our concept of subpersonalities is indeed well supported by objective tests.

GLOVER

But in philosophy the same thing has been happening. There is more than one region within the brain, more than one module of the brain. And these modules or agents are capable of acting independently. It must be possible, therefore, for there to be subpersonalities acting independently.

This argument has in recent years exercised several philosophers, who have discussed the difficulties involved in, for example, the hemisphere research. After reviewing a great deal of this recent philosophical argument, Jonathan Glover says that it is reasonable to see the disconnected right hemisphere of the split-brain patient as a centre of consciousness. If this is right, the experiments do demonstrate divided consciousness. So it must be possible to have separate modules, distinct subpersonalities, in the same person.

PARFIT

Similarly, after discussing a thought experiment where he had the power to separate the two halves of his brain at will, the philosopher Derek Parfit concludes by denying the necessary unity of consciousness. This idea of the necessary unity was laid down by Kant many years ago and has hardly been questioned since. As he says, what is a fact must be possible. And it is a fact that people with disconnected hemispheres have two separate streams of consciousness – two series of thoughts and experiences. Each of these is unaware of the other. Each of these two streams separately displays unity of consciousness. This may be a surprising fact, Parfit says, but we can understand it. We can come to believe that a person's mental history need not be like a canal with only one channel. It could be like a river, occasionally dividing and having separate streams.

He concludes that if all this is so, then we can also imagine what it would be like to divide and reunite our minds.

It is perhaps only because so much of this work is so recent that it is still not well known. What I have found is that people do not attempt to disprove the idea of subpersonalities, but simply to ignore it. For the most part psychologists who do not like the idea of subpersonalities simply organize things so that it is quite impossible for such a concept to emerge. They do not actually dispute it.

Chapter 24

Beyond the subpersonalities
The real self, the higher self and the soul

It must have been obvious that all the way through this discussion, we have been avoiding a certain area. It is now time to give that area some due attention.

What we have been avoiding is the whole question of whether there is anything beyond the subpersonalities. We have left it ambiguous as to whether there is such a thing as the Real Self, or the Higher Self (Transpersonal Self, Greater Self, Deeper Self, Inner Self, Self with a capital S, and so on), or whether there is such a thing as the soul.

In a way this is not a particularly important issue. There is plenty of work to be done, regardless of how we may wish to answer this question. But at the same time it would be cowardly not to admit that there is a real question here, even though it may be difficult to answer.

Most of the time we act and talk as if we were divided into two, like a horse and a rider. The mind is on top, like the rider, and the body and the emotions are down below, like the horse. This is the traditional way of seeing the matter, and it is taken for granted in much of our thinking and our literature.

THE REAL SELF

But through the process of self-understanding, in which the idea of subpersonalities has helped us, we become more integrated. We heal the many splits in the person, most particularly the split between mind and body. We sometimes use the word 'centaur' (the mythical being who was horse and rider in one) to describe the difference between the horse-and-rider separation of the previous stage and the unification which we may later reach.

At the earlier stage we tend to think of the mind as in charge of the body; the mind has to guide and discipline the body, as a rider guides and disciplines a horse. At the centaur stage the horse and the rider become one. At this level we have the experience of authenticity; a combination of self-respect and self-enactment. We cannot act in an authentic way until we reach this stage.

In other words, through the process of self-development, we get a great sense of unity, of being together with ourselves in a quite new way. We now have a real centre, so to speak. At first this may seem uncertain and shaky. But as time goes by we get more and more of a sense of this being solid and reliable.

So what has happened to the subpersonalities? After a while, I believe, we find that they are still there, even though they may have been transformed in various ways. But because we are now more sure of who the 'I' is, we actually have more freedom to move around between all the different 'Is' that there may be at different times and in different places. And this time we are doing it, not compulsively, but by choice. As someone put it, we have a number of houses to choose from, and can go into any house we want.

THE HIGHER SELF

And at this point we may see the possibility too of relating to a higher self (deeper self, inner self, greater self). One can ask directly to talk to the higher mind or one can lead a person into the higher mind through a meditative procedure. In dealing with the higher mind, we must be very careful that we do not confuse an inner Pusher with the actual spiritual energy. The real spiritual energy we call the higher self gives us a more removed point of view, not so immersed in the struggle. It gives a perspective. It does not solve problems (well, occasionally it does, but it is not to be depended on for that). It does not create pressure. Amazing insight can come from such parts of ourselves. When such a voice is contacted, a strong empowerment may take place. We are beginning to connect to inner sources of strength and wisdom.

One of the errors which can strike at this point is for someone to say that what we are talking about here is the superego, or the ego-ideal. The superego, as the voice of conscience, seems to come to us sometimes from outside, or as a still small voice from inside. And this may be very like, in some ways, the small voice from the higher self.

We can, however, make some important distinctions here. The higher self can be differentiated from the superego as follows:

Superego	Higher self
judgmental	compassionate
fearful	loving
opinionated	wise
intrusive	receptive
dominating	allowing
rationalizing	intuitive
controlled	spontaneous
restrictive	creative
conventional	inspired
anxious	peaceful
defensive	open
separated	connected
punitive	forgiving
critical	nurturing

One of the main differences we have to look at when considering this whole question of the higher self is the question of boundaries. What the ego, the superego and the real self have in common is that they all have strict boundaries. All the humanistic writers are very clear about this. 'I am I and you are you', and so forth. But at the stage where we genuinely get in touch with the higher self all this changes quite radically.

At this stage the separative identifications dissolve. We can take down the barriers which divide us from other people, and experience our common identity. If we can imagine a hilly country which sinks into the sea, leaving the peaks above the waves, we can easily imagine how the islands so formed could become very different, with different flora and fauna and different histories of invasion or cultivation. From many important and valid points of view, they are now separate and distinct. But if we look beneath the waves, we can see that they are still part of the same mainland, still the hills they always were, rising above a common plain. In just the same way, it is true to say that we are separate individuals: it is also true to say that we are members one of another, that we are all part of something greater; and this is what we realize and experience at the level of the higher self.

It is very important to realize that this is not a 'should' or an 'ought' – it is simply our experience at this stage. We have

reached it through our own changes, and not through taking on someone else's ideas.

THE SOUL

However, there is also another important caution here, which is a possible confusion with the idea of the soul. The higher self is not the same as the soul. The term *soul* is commonly used to designate only the simple subject of awareness of any level of consciousness. The soul, as simple subject of awareness, may be identified with any level of consciousness, whereas the higher self as witness is specifically to do with a higher stage of development beyond the real self.

In contrast to the transpersonal self, neither psyche nor soul designates a particular stage of development. The term *soul* is commonly used to refer to the subtle separate self-sense that travels the spiritual path through various realms of existence, and which is particularly hospitable to the imagination. The term *psyche* is more often used to refer to the ground of psychological self-awareness at any level on the spectrum of consciousness.

STAGES OF DEVELOPMENT

So there is a process of development with various stages on the way. And we have to say that there are real dangers in losing our way if we try to hurry on too fast without really knowing what we are doing. The ideal way to proceed is to do our therapy first, working through all the material to do with our subpersonalities. This enables us to find our centre, our real self. This gives us a secure base from which to go on, if we wish to, into the spiritual realms.

It seems to me that if we do not do this, we are going to move too fast into the higher-self area, and run real risks of very bad experiences. It is well known that people who experiment with the Ouija board in order to obtain psychic communications can experience some frightening encounters with 'bad psychic characters'. These entities as it were take the opportunity to play tricks and upset the applecart. These apparently discarnate entities may very often be just projections of our own nastiness. They may be our own disowned energies which we have not yet dealt with or come to terms with.

And more generally, it is all too easy for us to go into the apparently higher realms of the transpersonal carrying all the baggage of our unworked-out subpersonalities. These then by the process of projection become voices which inspire us or frighten us. In some lucky cases they may actually give us books, music, art works, spiritual communications and the like.

The recent excitement about channelling (drawing down information from discarnate entities of one kind or another) gives us many examples of this. One expert estimates that 85 per cent of these communications come straight from the personal unconscious of the person affected. Experienced channelling teachers are the first to tell us that most of what novices think is channelling is rather the product of self-delusion. Such errors are brought on as a result of psychic immaturity. Or, through a kind of self-hypnosis, some so-called channelling is simple imagination creating its own characters.

But some of it does come from the higher (transpersonal, deeper, greater, inner) self; it is important here, as elsewhere, not to make the mistake of saying that it is nothing but self-deception. We do not want a reductionist 'nothing but', but simply a sober realization that we are always subject to that which we have not dealt with in ourselves, whatever plane we may be on.

A good example of this came to my notice in the autobiography of a famous medium. She knew she had psychic abilities from an early age, and cultivated them, and became much in demand to demonstrate her powers. For several years she became more and more famous. And then one day, as she was coming down from the stage after a performance, she overheard two women talking, one of them saying that it was obvious that it had all been a cheat and a fake. This so upset her that she gave up the work, and became a nurse for five years. Now this is an example of how harmful it can be to omit doing your own therapy. If she had really worked through her own material properly, her ego would not have been so easily put down. She would have gone beyond the stage of depending upon other people's opinions in that way.

GLIMPSE EXPERIENCES

Over and over again it seems to be shown that unless we move from level to level in a sure and grounded way, we shall be subject to inflation and deflation. We have to be very aware that a glimpse of the higher-self level is perfectly valid, but is only a glimpse. We have to accept that a glimpse of any spiritual level we have not yet fully reached can be perfectly meaningful and important but only a glimpse.

This is one of the most important findings from the research which has been done in the area of spiritual development. Genuine glimpses of spiritual reality are quite common and very important when they do occur. But they can lead to spiritual inflation, a quite disastrous occurrence which makes us think we have got much further along the road than we really have. We go around collecting followers and thinking that we are really advanced. Usually this is illusory, or at least partial.

DISCERNMENT

And, of course, particular temptation arises from the idea of channelling, because in channelling we do not say, 'I am the spiritual being'. We make the apparently much more modest statement: 'I am the humble and unworthy channel through which this spiritual being communicates.' However, I suggest that we apply here exactly the same thinking that we saw in the case of subpersonalities generally, and take responsibility for our voices. No matter what the voice says, it is still my business what I do about it.

Discernment is called for, whether the intuited material comes from one's own unconscious or from beyond oneself. One must look the gift horse in the mouth in each case, and one must do this regardless of source. All the most reliable people in this field tell us not to accept messages just because of their seeming otherworldly status. Test what we tell you against experience and weigh it within, they say.

So in other words, we have to take it that it is us doing it, in just the same way as we saw before that we could not use subpersonalities as an excuse for our actions. Even if it really is the highest possible source giving us messages, that still does not excuse us from the duty of deciding what to do about it.

CONCLUSION

In the end it seems wisest to say that it may sometimes be useful to think of ourselves as a single unit, a cohesive self; it may sometimes be useful to think of ourselves as constituted of many parts, each with an identity of its own; it may sometimes be useful to think of ourselves as essentially spiritual beings; and it may sometimes be useful to think of ourselves as part of a greater whole. All of these are true, simultaneously and at all times.

So our conclusion must be that, while at certain stages unity may be very tempting and even apparently necessary, in the end multiplicity is just as real and just as important, all the way down the line. There never comes a time when we can simply abandon our multiplicity and lay down in a perfect and final unity. We may not have subpersonalities in the sense that they fight with one another, but we shall still have many angles, many colours, many quirks. We shall still be human.

Further reading

If this book interested you, you can follow up the ideas here:

Beahrs, J.O. (1982) *Unity and Multiplicity: Multilevel Consciousness of Self in Hypnosis, Psychiatric Disorder and Mental Health*, New York: Brunner/Mazel.
A very interesting discussion by a hypnotherapist. Sophisticated and far-reaching.
Berne, E. (1972) *What Do You Say After You Say Hello?*, New York: Grove Press.
Tells you about the Parent, Adult and Child, about scripts and the rest.
Bolen, J.S. (1985) *Goddesses in Everywoman*, New York: Harper & Row.
A useful book by a Jungian on some common archetypes and how they work. The importance of mythology and what it can mean to us.
Ferrucci, P. (1982) *What We May Be*, Wellingborough: Turnstone Press.
Contains a good chapter on subpersonalities.
Hillman, J. (1975) *Re-visioning Psychology*, New York: Harper & Row.
Contains the basic argument about personification. Hillman is very sophisticated – one of the key modern Jungians.
Johnson, R. (1986) *Inner Work*, San Francisco: Harper.
One of the best books for telling you how to work with subpersonalities.
Minsky, M. (1988) *The Society of Mind*, London: Pan.
A very well-written discussion of hardware and software.
O'Connor, E. (1971) *Our Many Selves*, New York: Harper & Row.
A beautiful book if you can find it.
Ornstein, R. (1986) *MultiMinds*, Boston, MA: Houghton Mifflin.
Very clear and interesting example of one particular theory.
Redfearn, J.W.T. (1985) *My Self, My Many Selves*, London: Academic Press.
A quite advanced and difficult account by a Jungian.
Rowan, J. (1990) *Subpersonalities: The People Inside Us*, London: Routledge.
The best and fullest account yet, giving chapter and verse for everything described in the current volume.

Satir, V. (1978) *Your Many Faces*, Berkeley, CA: Celestial Arts.
   A delightful little book, very readable.
Sliker, G. (1992) *Multiple Mind*, Boston, MA: Shambhala.
   The very latest word, from another Jungian. Looks very good.
Stone, H. and Winkelman, S. (1989) *Embracing Our Selves*, San Rafael, CA:
   New World Library.
   The standard work from the Voice Dialogue people, very well done.
Watkins, J. (1978) *The Therapeutic Self*, New York: Human Sciences Press.
   Quite heavy and technical, a book for therapists.
Watkins, M. (1986) *Invisible Guests: The Development of Internal Dialogues*,
   Hillsdale, NJ: The Analytic Press.
   A beautiful book, making some very important and fascinating
   points.

Index